The Political Economy of the Asia Pacific

Series Editor

Vinod K. Aggarwal

More information about this series at http://www.springer.com/series/7840

Jongwon Choi · Huck-ju Kwon
Min Gyo Koo

Editors

The Korean Government
and Public Policies
in a Development Nexus

Sustaining Development and Tackling Policy
Changes – Volume 2

 Springer

Editors
Jongwon Choi
Graduate School of Public Administration
Seoul National University
Seoul
South Korea

Min Gyo Koo
Graduate School of Public Administration
Seoul National University
Seoul
South Korea

Huck-ju Kwon
Graduate School of Public Administration
Seoul National University
Seoul
South Korea

ISSN 1866-6507
The Political Economy of the Asia Pacific
ISBN 978-3-319-52472-6 (hardcover)
ISBN 978-3-319-66346-3 (softcover)
DOI 10.1007/978-3-319-52473-3

ISSN 1866-6515 (electronic)

ISBN 978-3-319-52473-3 (eBook)

Library of Congress Control Number: 2016963419

Printed on acid-free paper

This Springer imprint is published by Springer Nature
The registered company is Springer International Publishing AG
The registered company address is: Gewerbestrasse 11, 6330 Cham, Switzerland

Foreword

The question of how countries escape the middle-income trap is a pressing issue for many governments throughout the world. For neoliberal economists, with a belief in the miracle of the unfettered market, the answer is simple: keep the state out of business, and everything will be fine. But with a backlash against globalization growing throughout both the developed and developing world, this answer is not only facile but also a recipe for disaster. Those who understand the political economy of development, rather than the fantasy of apolitical growth, will applaud the publication of this book. By shedding light on both the successes and failures of state intervention as the Korean government has sought to promote Korea's rise toward new economic heights, this volume makes an important contribution to our understanding of both the Korean economy and important lessons for other countries.

This book, a companion volume to *The Korean Government and Public Policy in Development Nexus* by Huck-ju Kwon and Min Gyo Koo published in 2014, takes the story of Korea's development to the present. Its focus on the critical problems faced by Korea in the wake of the 1997–1998 financial crisis, and the government's response and interaction with societal groups sheds light on the complexity of promoting development. The need to address the problems of losers from increasing globalization through the creation of a more significant welfare state and the difficulties in promoting advanced industries rather than simply catching up to more developed countries are essential elements in Korea's development story. Given that Korea was also able to consolidate its democratic institutions after the transformation to civilian rule in the late 1980s, its success demonstrates the fallacy of the need for an authoritarian government to promote successful industrial policies. By focusing on the interaction between the civil society and the state apparatus in the face of critical challenges, this book goes beyond just a single case study of Korea to deepen our knowledge of transition political economy.

By systematically showing both the benefits and costs of government intervention, as well as the political coalition building process necessary to sustain development, this book provides a balanced approach to understanding the role of the state in economic development. Today, Korea faces a critical challenge from anti-globalization sentiment that can endanger its development strategy. As a highly trade-dependent country without the market size of China or India, emphasizing only the domestic market is simply not tenable. Moreover, unlike most countries seeking to improve its economic standing, South Korea also faces the relatively unique problem of an extremely hostile North Korea. Moreover, with a potential of increasing competition in trade, finance, and security between China and the USA, as a middle power country, Korea must carefully calibrate both its foreign political and economy policy. As the contributors and editors clearly show, "success" can never be final. There is no "end of history" for Korea—or for other countries for that matter. By illuminating the interplay of politics and economics, this book provides a welcome and innovative contribution to both theory and policy about development. As the series editor, I congratulate the editors on a masterful work.

Vinod K. Aggarwal
Travers Family Senior Faculty Fellow and
Professor, Political Science, Affiliated Professor,
Haas School of Business,
Director, Berkeley APEC Study Center
Berkeley, CA, USA

The original version of the book was revised:
The volume number in the cover and title page
has been updated. The erratum to the book is
available at 10.1007/978-3-319-52473-3_10

Contents

Editors and Contributors

About the Editors

Jongwon Choi is a professor at Graduate School of Public Administration, and Director of the Asia Development Institute, Seoul National University. He graduated from Seoul National University (B.A. in Economics in 1982 and M.P.A. in 1984) and obtained Ph.D. in public policy from University of Michigan in 1989. He was the dean of Graduate School of Public Administration (2008–2010). Previously, he worked for Economic Planning Board (EPB) and Korea Development Institute (KDI). He was a non-standing commissioner of Korean Fair Trade Commission, Republic of Korea (2008–2011). He also was the chairman of Korean Public Enterprise Evaluation Committee (2012–2013). He is the president of the Korean Society of Public Enterprises since 2009. He was the editor of the Korean Public Administration Review. His research interest is on policy-making and policy implementation theories and empirical studies. His publications include "James G. March and Policy Studies in Korea" (Korean Policy Studies Journal, 2014), "On ICT Governance and Regulation" (ICT Forum, 2014), "Institutional Leadership and Perceived Performance: Evidence from the Korean Minister Survey" (Korean Journal of Policy Studies, 2011), Consumers and the Rule of Law (Seoul National University Press, 2008, co-author), Korean National Governance System: Challenges and Strategies (Seoul: Nanam, 2008, co-author). Email: jwchoi@snu.ac.kr

Huck-ju Kwon is a professor at the Graduate School of Public Administration, and Deputy Director of the Asia Development Institute, Seoul National University. He is also the editor of *the Korean Public Administration Review* and co-editor of *Global Social Policy* (Sage). His research interest is on comparative social policy in East Asia, international development policy, and global governance. He was the director of the Global Research Network on Social Protection in East Asia, funded by the Korea Research Council (2010–2013), and visiting scholar at the Harvard Yenching Institute (2013–2014). Previously, he worked as the research coordinator at the

United Nations Research Institute for Social Development (UNRISD) (2002–2005). His publications include "Poverty Reduction and Good Governance" (*Development and Change*, 2014), *Transforming the Developmental Welfare State in East Asia* (Palgrave, 2005), *The East Asian Welfare Model: the State and Welfare Orientalism* (London: Routledge, 1998, co-author), and *the Korean State and Social Policy* (Oxford University Press, 2011). E-mail: hkwon4@snu.ac.kr

Min Gyo Koo is an associate professor in the Graduate School of Public Administration at Seoul National University in Korea. His research interests include East Asian political economy and maritime affairs. Among his many publications is *Island Disputes and Maritime Regime Building in East Asia: Between a Rock and a Hard Place* (2010, Springer). Aside from many book chapters, he has published his research in a wide range of journals, including *International Relations of the Asia-Pacific*, *The Pacific Review*, *Pacific Affairs*, *Asian Perspective*, *European Journal of East Asia Studies*, and *Journal of East Asian Studies*. He has also co-edited (with Vinod K. Aggarwal) *Asia's New Institutional Architecture: Evolving Structures for Managing Trade, Financial, and Security Relations* (2008, Springer). From fall 2005 to spring 2007, he served as a postdoctoral fellow at the Center for International Studies and as a full-time lecturer in the School of International Relations at the University of Southern California. He also taught at Yonsei University in Korea from fall 2007 to spring 2010. He served as 2015–2016 Harvard–Yenching Scholar at Harvard University. Email: mgkoo@snu.ac.kr

Contributors

Taehyon Choi is an associate professor at the Graduate School of Public Administration, Seoul National University. His research interests include deliberation and decision making, new governance, and public participation. His papers appear in journals including *International Public Management Journal, Journal of Public Administration Research and Theory, Public Administration Review, Korean Public Administration Review, and Korean Policy Studies Review*. He is also a co-author of three books regarding institutional changes in the Korean government and collaborative governance. He received several academic awards including the Carlo Masini Award for Innovative Scholarship (Academy of Management 2010 Annual Meeting). He serves as an editorial board member of *Korean Journal of Public Administration* and *Korean Society and Public Administration*. He taught at the University of Hawaii at Manoa and has served as visiting scholar at the University of Southern California. E-mail: taehyon@snu.ac.kr

Junhee Han is a Ph.D. in Economics at Seoul National University, Korea. He received B.A. in Economics at University of British Columbia, Canada, and M.A. in Economics at Seoul National University. His research interest includes international trade, macro-policy, and agent-based modeling. E-mail: kairass@snu.ac.kr

Buru Im is a Ph.D. candidate in Economics at Seoul National University and research associate of Capital Economic Consulting Group, Lee & Ko. He received B.A. and M.A. in Economics at Seoul National University. His research interest is on the empirical analysis of latecomer's catch-up at the firm level with an emphasis on the technological capability and strategic behaviors. Email: imburu@snu.ac.kr

Keun Lee is a professor of Economics at the Seoul National University, and the director of the Center for Economic Catch-up. He has been awarded the 2014 Schumpeter Prize for his monograph on *Schumpeterian Analysis of Economic Catch-up: Knowledge, Path-creation and the Middle Income Trap* (2013 Cambridge Univ. Press) by the International Schumpeter Society. He is also the president-elect of this Society. He is a member of the Committee for Development Policy of UN, a co-editor of Research Policy, and a member of the governing board of Globelics. He obtained Ph.D. degree from the University of California, Berkeley, and worked before at the World Bank, University of Aberdeen, and the East–West Center. Email: kenneth@snu.ac.kr

Yeonho Lee is a professor of political science in the Department of Political Science and International Studies, and director of Yonsei-EU Jean Monnet Centre of Excellence, Yonsei University, Seoul, Korea. He received his B.A. in political science at Yonsei University, Korea. He read political science at the University of Cambridge, UK, with the support of the Chevening Scholarship, and obtained M. Phil. and Ph.D. He had been an ESRC Fellow at the University of Warwick, UK, until he joined in Yonsei in 1998. His research and teaching interests include international development cooperation and EU, development theories and the Korean political economy. He is the author of *The State, Society and Big Business in South Korea*, Routledge and *Theories of Development*, Yonsei University Press, *Unequal Development and Democracy in South Korea*, Pakyongsa. He has also published several articles in academic journals including *the Pacific Review*, *Asian Survey*, and *Korean Political Science Review*. Email: yhlee@yonsei.ac.kr

Byoung Kwon Sohn is a professor at Department of Political Science and International Relations, Chung-Ang University. His research interest is on comparative political process, American foreign policy, and Korea–USA relationship, with an emphasis on the domestic sources of foreign policy. He was a Fulbright Visiting Scholar to the Department of Political Science at the University of Iowa (2011–2012), vice president of Korean Political Science Association (2013), president of Korean Association of Party Studies (2013), and dean of the Graduate School of International Studies at Chung-Ang University (2013–2014). His publications include *Climate Change and the Dilemma for the U.S. Hegemony* (Seoul: Sogang University Press, 2012), *Democratic Deepening in Korea: Institutional Development and Challenges* (Seoul: Oreum, 2012, co-author), and "Changes in Asia and China Strategies of the U.S. and Korea's U.S. Strategy Options" in *East Asia and the Korean Peninsula in the Sino-US Rivalry* (Seoul: Nulpoon Plus, 2015). Email: byoungk@chol.com

Chi Hoon Sung is a Ph.D. candidate in political science and international studies at Yonsei University. He received B.A. in Civil Engineering and M.A. in Political Science from the same university. His research interest includes party politics and elections in Korea. Email: summits83@naver.com

Chapter 1
Introduction

Jongwon Choi, Huck-ju Kwon and Min Gyo Koo

1.1 The Goal of the Book

Korea has made great progress from one of the poorest countries in the world toward becoming an affluent industrial society during the last fifty years. Korea was also very successful in terms of democratic transition, experiencing a number of governmental transitions without any serious political instability for the last thirty years, despite the recent political scandals surrounding President Park Geun-hye. Korean society has also passed through several critical cross-junctures at which other developing societies failed to consolidate past achievements in economic and social development.

The Korean transition poses three important questions for us to answer in terms of development theory as well as policy implications for other developing and middle-income countries: first, as one of the poorest countries, how was Korea able to leap forward in economic and social development? Second, how did Korea come through political transition from an authoritarian regime to a democratic polity while also overcoming serious economic challenges such as the East Asian economic crisis in 1997/1998? Third and lastly, will Korea be able to sustain the consolidation of its economic and social achievements to become a leader in the global community?

These questions are pertinent not only for scholars and policy makers interested in Korean public policy, but also for international observers, especially those concerned with social and economic development in their own countries.

J. Choi (✉) · H. Kwon · M.G. Koo
Graduate School of Public Administration, Seoul National University, Seoul, South Korea
e-mail: jwchoi@snu.ac.kr

H. Kwon
e-mail: hkwon4@snu.ac.kr

M.G. Koo
e-mail: mgkoo@snu.ac.kr

© Springer International Publishing AG 2017
J. Choi et al. (eds.), *The Korean Government and Public Policies in a Development Nexus*, The Political Economy of the Asia Pacific, DOI 10.1007/978-3-319-52473-3_1

Development remains an elusive challenge for many developing countries. No less than one billion people in the world either suffer from poverty or are exposed to high risk of poverty (Collier 2007; World Bank 2016). This is why the Korean development experience in general and public policy in particular are of such great interest to policy makers in developing countries. It is true that there has been a large body of literature on this topic. The majority, however, is concerned with economic development and does not give adequate attention to the functioning of the government, despite the fact that the developmental state is recognized as playing a crucial role in the process.

The first volume in the series, *The Korean Government and Public Policies in a Development Nexus* (Kwon and Koo 2014), addressed this question with a focus on the inner-working of the developmental state and areas of public policy such as education, social protection and international trade. Although under the regime of the developmental state the government single-mindedly carried out public policies to stimulate economic growth, we argued in this volume that public policies were affected and changed by the process. It was a two-way interaction between Korean society and the government. The Korean government adopted policy as new challenges arose in the course of development, while simultaneously leading development efforts.

Nevertheless, pulling a country out of poverty is quite a different process from the further step of pushing through the middle-income threshold. Many developing countries were caught in the middle-income trap after initial progress in economic and social development. For instance, Argentina in South America made impressive progress in the 1960s, but failed to consolidate what had been achieved and to make headway on the path to mature development. There are many other countries which have never been able to overcome the middle-income trap, and this could have contemporary implications for China, Vietnam, and India in the wake of rapid economic success.

There are many reasons why countries with initial success in economic devel-opment cannot sustain progress and fail to push through the middle-income threshold. At some point after experiencing steady industrial growth, the supply of cheap rural labor in developing countries runs out, which is called as Lewis Turning Point (Ranis 2004). At this point in time, developing countries can no longer rely on industrial development based on cheap labor. Trade union movements emerge and political pressure for equitable redistribution mounts. Social and political conflicts can also disrupt development. Military coup d'états in many Latin American countries in the 1980s derailed the development process, while the recent experi-ences of political revolution and civil war in the Middle East and North Africa show how fragile development can be.

In the early 1980s and the late 1990s, Korea also experienced political and economic crises during which it might have been easy to fall off course (Chang 1998; Haggard and Moon 1990). Nevertheless, Korea navigated the challenges and is now contemplating further progress. How could Korea overcome the middle-income trap? Economic development from the middle of the 1980s through the 1990s and 2000s has been quite impressive; almost as impressive, if not more so, as it was from the 1960s to the 1970s. During this period, there were two historic milestones in terms of political and economic development. In 1987, the military-turned-leader of the governing party made a political concession for democratization so that the President would be elected by popular vote. It was simultaneously the result of rigorous political campaigning for democratization through civil movements since the 1970s, and a political compromise between the military-conservative coalition and political movements for democratization. It also signified huge political uncertainty for the future.

Another critical juncture for the Korean transition was the East Asian economic crisis, during which the Korean economy was on the brink of financial collapse. To steer away from the crisis, it was necessary to implement economic reform as well as public sector reform. Every aspect of the policy paradigm that had worked effectively during the previous era was questioned by the International Monetary Fund as well as Korean policy stakeholders. The developmental state in general and the role of the bureaucrats in particular were critically assessed.

1.2 An Overview of the Book

With hindsight, we know that Korea has experienced and successfully navigated turbulent times, but the public policies and theoretical underpinnings adopted by stakeholders and the Korean government remain to be analyzed. In this book, we will try to answer the question as to how Korea was able to overcome challenges of political and economic crisis and to push through the middle-income threshold. More specifically, we will look into periods 2 and 3 (see Fig. 1.1) rather than period 1,

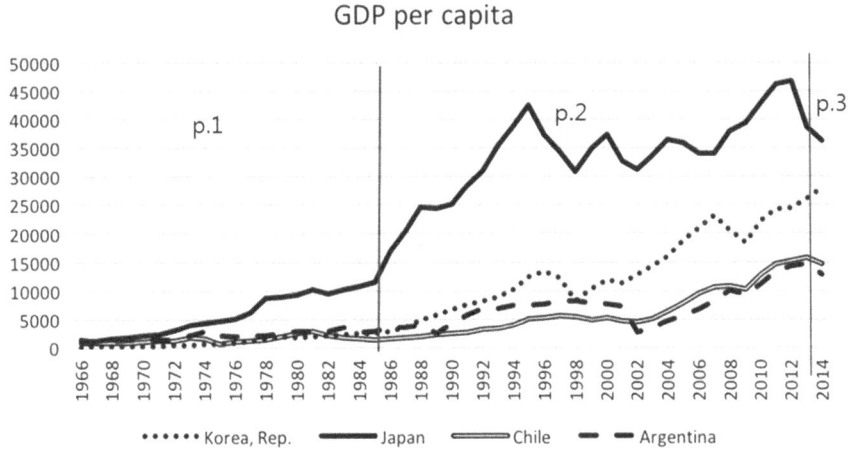

Fig. 1.1 Long-term development trends in comparison. *Note* Values are in current US$. *Source* World development indicators (http://databank.worldbank.org/data)

which has already been the subject of much previous research. We will examine whether the developmental state paradigm was replaced or revised as the rationale of public policy in period 2, and address the question of whether or not Korea has envisioned a new idea for the next phase of development (period 3) in which citizen rights and individual creativity are more recognized and respected.

In particular, in Part I we will examine the changing policy environment within which stakeholders and the Korean government operate, as well as the governance paradigm that the government attempted to establish as the main rationale for public policy. In Chap. 2, Jongwon Choi and Taehyun Choi will examine the economic, social and political environment of public policies in Korea since the late 1980s. Their starting point is that the success of public policy is contingent on its consistency with the policy environment, and hence changes in the policy environment pose challenges for policy makers. This chapter also provides an introduction to the macro economic and social structure of society for the following chapters. In Chap. 3 on changes in the rationale of governance, Huck-ju Kwon traces back the policy efforts of the successive Korean governments to replace the developmental state as the rationale of governance after democratization. Although the Korean governments after democratization maintained that the policy regime of the developmental state should be replaced with a kind of liberal regime, Kwon questions whether the Korean government conceived a new idea of governance. In Chap. 4, Yeonho Lee and Chi Hoon Sung examines the rise of civil society organizations and their changing role in the relationship between the state and society since the late 1980s. Compared to the policy regime of the developmental state, civil society organizations were much more involved in policy making and implementation, with a rapid increase in the number of organizations and participating members. Lee compares the civil society movements in subsequent governments, notably under the progressive governments of Kim Dae-jung and Roh Moo-hyun, as well as subsequent conservative governments. Lee questions whether civil society organizations became independent from state interference, despite growth in numbers and influence.

In Part II, this book includes chapters dealing with specific public policy areas: national innovation policy, social policy, trade policy, and foreign policy. In Chap. 5, Keun Lee, Buru Im and Junhee Han describes the evolution of the national innovation system in Korea during the catch-up and post catch-up periods. Technical upgrade and diversification have been identified as main strategies for graduation from the middle-income class. Lee explains the characteristics of innovation activities in Korea and elaborates how technological advancement contributed to Korea's economic progress, but questions whether the past strategy of innovation can bring Korea's competitive edge to the next level.

One of the salient features of public policy in Korea during the middle-income period is the expansion of the social protection system, which Huck-ju Kwon calls the developmental welfare state. This refers to a welfare state arranged to be instrumental for economic development. In Chap. 6, Kwon explains the expansion of the developmental welfare state in the wake of the Asian economic crisis. He argues that such expansion was critical to maintaining social cohesion during the period of painful structural adjustment, as well as facilitating economic and public sector reforms. Kwon maintains that it will be necessary to transform the developmental welfare state into a universal welfare state to meet the social demands of post-industrial society, but he questions whether or not the Korean government has a clear idea about policy directions for the future of the welfare state.

Chapters 7 and 8 deal with public policies regarding the international dimension. In Chap. 7, Min Gyo Koo examines Korean trade policy in the context of the changing internal and international trade environment in the wake of the East Asian economic crisis. In particular, he carefully analyzes trade policy change using the notions of repositioning, adapting and restructuring. He raises doubt about Korea's ability to meet the dual demands of democracy and trade openness. In Chap. 8, Byoung Kwon Sohn identifies foreign policy challenges for Korea in the context of East Asia in light of an increasingly globalized world and post-democratization. He explains the dynamics of democratic politics in which governments can no longer monopolize information regarding international relations or foreign policy decisions. On the international scene, Korea is in a tenuous position between China on one side and the US and Japan on the other side, while North Korea continually poses a nuclear security threat.

Throughout the book, each chapter in some way analyzes how Korea has weathered policy challenges after democratization and the East Asian economic crisis. At the same time, however, the authors of each chapter have one crucial question in mind: will Korea be able to consolidate its economic and social achievements over the last six decades, and transition into a fully mature post-industrial society and leader of the global community? Our readers, of course, will come up with their own thoughts on this question, and it will be discussed further in the conclusion.

References

Chang H (1998) Korea: the misunderstood crisis. World Dev 26(8):1555–1561
Collier P (2007) The bottom billion: why the poorest countries are failing and what can be done about it. Oxford University Press, Oxford
Haggard S, Moon CI (1990) Institutions and economic policy: theory and a Korean case study. World Polit 42(2):210–237
Kwon H, Koo MG (2014) The Korean government and public policies in a development nexus, vol 1. Springer, New York
Ranis G (2004) Arthur Lewis' contribution to development thinking and policy, Yale University. Economic growth center discussion paper series
World Bank (2016) Poverty & equity data

Part I
Policy Environment and Governance

Chapter 2
Changes in the Political, Social and Economic Environment of Public Policy in South Korea After the 1980s

Jongwon Choi and Taehyon Choi

2.1 Introduction

Any open system can survive only when it serves the need of the upper system, or its environment (Robertson and Choi 2010). Public policy is a way for government to respond to input from civil society, which forms the environment of the government. To put it another way, public policy decisions cannot be aptly understood from a closed system perspective; that is, from a perspective that focuses only on the internal structure and process of government. Instead, public policy can be better understood from an open system perspective that considers the policy environment as playing a major role. The environment, when appropriately understood, can explain much about why a policy is or is not adopted, implemented, and revised.

The purpose of this chapter is to provide an overview of policy environment changes in South Korea after the 1980s. We assume that the current public policy in South Korea can be better understood by analyzing the changes in the political, social, and economic environment of public policy. We take a historical perspective to analyze the institutional setting of the Korean state. To do so, we pay attention to two critical events in the contemporary history of the development of South Korea. One is the 6/29 declaration in 1987, which led to democratization of the country. The other is the financial crisis in 1997, which led to neo-liberal reforms all around

J. Choi (✉) · T. Choi
Graduate School of Public Administration, Seoul National University, Seoul, South Korea
e-mail: jwchoi@snu.ac.kr

T. Choi
e-mail: taehyon@snu.ac.kr

© Springer International Publishing AG 2017
J. Choi et al. (eds.), *The Korean Government and Public Policies in a Development Nexus*, The Political Economy of the Asia Pacific,
DOI 10.1007/978-3-319-52473-3_2

the country. We argue that these two events left an imprinting effect on public policy, and changed the path of state development afterward. We contend that political, social, and economic changes during the period are all intertwined, drive key policy actors to a certain direction, and are in turn affected by actor responses.

Although we discuss a lot of political, social, and economic events around and after the two major events, our goal is not to provide a comprehensive perspective to understand those events in the form of political theory or ideology. Instead, our main purpose is to identify key events or indicators that demonstrate how the state and society have changed, thus providing the background knowledge on which to base a better understanding of the current policy issues in South Korea. It is noteworthy, however, that our general discussion benefits from the developmental state theory and the theory of the variety of capitalism (for details, see Evans 1995; Hall and Soskice 2001; Johnson 1982; Weiss 1998; Woo-Cumings 1999), which are in the tradition of historical institutionalism. Although we do not attempt to verify or falsify those models, they are used to frame the discussion of political, social, and economic changes and challenges.

We begin by discussing the policy environment during the Third to the Fifth Republic, which can be characterized as the developmental era of South Korea. Next we review the background and content of the 6/29 declaration and the financial crisis in 1997 respectively. We then analyze in more detail changes in the policy environment according to its political, social, and economic dimensions, and discuss how those changes in the policy environment affected key policy actors: presidents, legislature, and state bureaucracy. Finally, we conclude this chapter by summarizing the discussion and proposing some speculation on the future of the Korean state.

2.2   Overview of the Contemporary History of South Korea

2.2.1   Political Environment During the Developmental Era

To understand the policy environment today, we need to rely on a historical view of the institutionalization of the political sector in South Korea. Before the key political turn of the 6/29 declaration in 1987, South Korea had experienced more than two decades of authoritarian regime since 1961. This period covers the time from the Third to the Fifth Republic when the Korean economy had grown rapidly but civil society had not fully grown into a democracy. The period was the heyday of the Korean developmental state or the East Asian "coordinated market economy" (Hall and Soskice 2001). Three key political situations can be highlighted.

First, the central government of the Korean state in this era institutionalized a typical developmental state. There are two key features of this state institutional-ization: political elites that pursued the state development, and bureaucratic elites that provided professional resources for economic growth in response to political elites. The Park Chung-hee administration focused on economic development by designing and implementing state-driven economic development plans, establishing modern capitalist markets, strategically supporting key corporations (which later grew into *chaebols*) to grow fast, and suppressing political and labor rights movements (Bedeski 1994; Heo and Roehrig 2010). The administration's goal was realized by competent, coherent, and compliant state bureaucracy (Johnson 1982).

Second, civil society had not emerged yet to exercise democratic control over the government. Although the civil society experienced major success toward democracy through the 4/19 Movement in 1960, it still remained relatively weak and under-organized compared to the state, which was typical among newly independent countries (Alavi 1979). Nevertheless, this era of economic development and authoritarian regime is not characterized simply by a ruling government versus a ruled civil society. As we analyze in detail in the next sections, this era of authoritarian regime also embedded potential for democracy, including the rise of the middle class, a growing number of civic organizations, organization of labor and student movements, and increased autonomy of large firms.

Finally, it is worth mentioning briefly the effect of the cold war and economic boom in the Western countries during the second half of the 20th century, which provided the Korean state with a favorable global market (Woo-Cumings 1999). Along with the existence of political elites that pursued the development of a strong state and the existence of competent and coherent state bureaucracy, the generous global market condition enriched the soil for South Korea to develop and grow quickly.

2.2.2   6/29 Declaration and Revision of Constitution: A Critical Juncture for Democratization

The first critical juncture that came with the end of the era of rapid economic development driven and managed by the authoritarian regime happened in 1987, when the 6/29 declaration was announced by Roh Tae-woo under the Chun Doo-hwan administration. The 6/29 declaration and the following constitutional revision made a significant imprinting effect on the institutionalization of political conditions afterward.

The 6/29 declaration was not an abrupt event initiated by political elite whim, but was their reluctant response to pressure from civil society. The increasing demand for more democracy that includes the 5/18 democratic uprising at Gwangju in 1980 and following civic movements against the authoritarian government hit a peak when the 6/10 civic uprising occurred in June 1987. The 6/29 declaration was a response by the authoritarian regime to propose a wide range of democratic reforms.

The 6/29 declaration initiated by Roh Tae-woo, then the delegate of the ruling party, included several significant reforms.[1] First, the direct presidential election system was proposed: "The constitution should be expeditiously amended, …, to adopt a direct presidential system, and presidential elections should be held under a new constitution to realize a peaceful change of government in February 1988." In addition, the declaration emphasized fairness and justness of election management.[2] The following constitution also reduced the length of the presidential term from seven to five years with no consecutive terms of service. However, this political achievement stemmed from narrow political negotiation among the ruling party and the opponent parties, and has therefore been criticized as not reflecting the diverse demands of citizens. Scholars have pointed out that excessive focus on the issue of the presidential term led to neglect of the other democratization agendas (Choi 2002).

Second, the declaration included the restoration of political prisoners' rights for the sake of "national reconciliation and unity." Prisoners included Kim Dae-jung, but excluded some "who have committed treason and have shaken the national foundations." The declaration states: "Mr. Kim Dae-jung should be amnestied and his civil rights restored. … At the same time, all those who are being detained in connection with the political situation should also be set free." This clause also stated that "antagonisms and confrontations must be resolutely eradicated," which is impressive as it indicated that the major issues at that moment did not simply involve institutional settings but also people's perceptions and social integration.

Third, the declaration emphasized the enhancement of basic human rights: "Human dignity must be respected even more greatly and the basic rights of citizens should be promoted and protected to the maximum." Furthermore, freedom of the press was to be restored by abolishing the Basic Press Act. The declaration also particularly mentioned the autonomy of local government and higher education institutions. Finally, the declaration called for a "clean and honest society" and the eradication of crimes against life and property.

The 6/29 declaration was followed by a major revision of the Constitution. The new Constitution was a significant turn from the authoritarian regime to a democratic one by strengthening the authority of the legislature and the judicial branch, constraining the power of the president, recovering local government autonomy, and ensuring basic human rights. After the 6/29 declaration, South Korea experienced two peaceful turnovers of political power in 1998 and 2008, and civil rights have been expanded to an unprecedented level.

---

[1]The English quotes from the 6/29 declaration in this chapter are based on Bedeski's work (1994).

[2]"… it is necessary also to revise the Presidential Election Law so that freedom of candidacy and fair competition are guaranteed … A revised election law should ensure maximum fairness and justness in election management, from the campaigns to the casting, opening and counting of ballots."

2.2.3 Financial Crisis and Kim Dae-Jung Administration Reforms: Another Critical Juncture

The second critical juncture after the authoritarian developmental state regime was the financial crisis in 1997. The financial crisis was not a one-time event, but rather an ongoing ordeal not visible to the public until the Kim Young-sam administration announced that South Korea would receive International Monetary Fund (IMF) bail-out money on November 21, 1997. The dawn of the crisis can be found in the change of foreign exchange rates and foreign exchange reserves. Figure 2.1 shows the worsening ratio between short-term foreign debt and foreign reserves until 1997. This broken balance between foreign debt and reserve was reflected in the foreign exchange rate. Figure 2.2 shows how rapidly the foreign exchange rate soared around November 1997.

On December 3, 1997, South Korea signed the MOU with the IMF for a bail-out to prevent the country from moratorium. The government received a conditional loan from the IMF of about 20 billion dollars. The per capita GDP plummeted from 12,000 dollars in 1996 to 7,300 dollars right after the crisis. The economic growth rate decreased from 4.7 to −6.9%, and the national credit rating (S&P index) declined from AA− to B+ (10 grades lower). In 1998, about 22 thousand firms went bankrupt, and the unemployment rate soared up to 7%.[3] In return for the conditional loan, South Korea agreed to implement neo-liberal reforms and austerity measures including high interest rates, high foreign exchange rates, and a reduced public budget. Comprehensive structural reforms of the domestic market were also implemented. Eventually, this was a huge departure from the old economic regime. After the crisis, the real GDP growth rate has never recovered as shown in Fig. 2.3.

With its inauguration in February 1998, the Kim Dae-jung administration announced four major reforms to overcome the financial crisis: financial market, corporate governance, labor market, and public sector. The reforms were partly a response to the IMF's conditional loan, but they were also what the former administrations attempted to accomplish (Ji 2011; Lim and Jang 2006). In a nutshell, they aimed at the enhancement of competitiveness in the private and the public sectors.

The financial market reform focused on the M&A of banks, the raising of public funds, and the improvement of financial regulation. For example, major banks such as Kookmin Bank and Korea Housing and Commercial Bank were forced to merge to ensure competence. In this process, public funds up to 160 trillion KRW flowed into financial institutes, dropping the ratio of insolvent obligations from 13.6 to 4%.[4]

Along with the financial market reform, the corporate governance reform aimed at disbanding insolvent enterprises, restructuring *chaebol* ownership structures, and

---

[3]http://news.naver.com/main/read.nhn?mode=LSD&mid=sec&sid1=117&oid=078&aid=000003 7944.2007.11.9.

[4]http://www.polinews.co.kr/news/article.html?no=11330.2001.3.1.

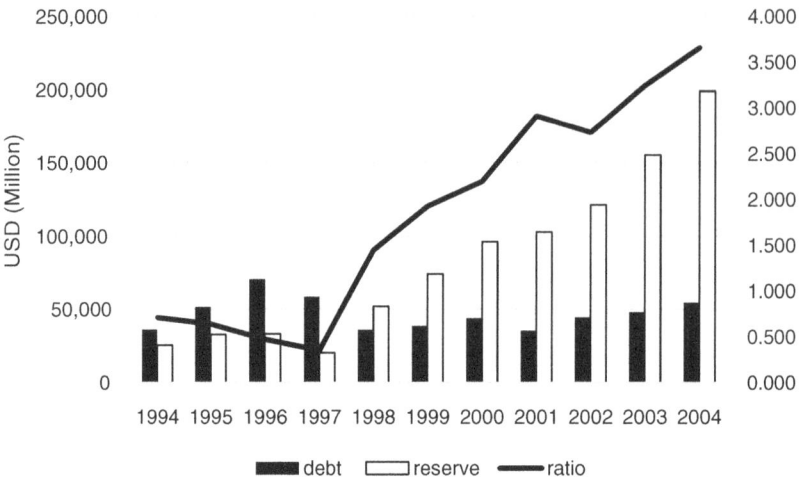

Fig. 2.1 Ratio between short-term foreign debt and foreign reserves. *Source* Bank of Korea (http://www.bok.or.kr)

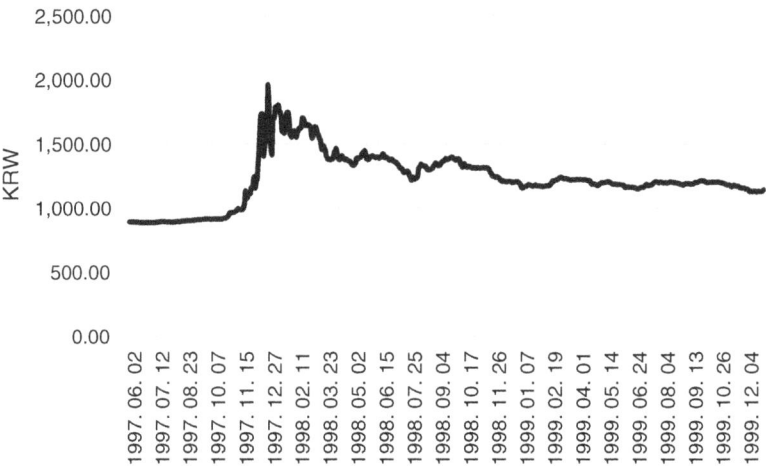

Fig. 2.2 Foreign exchange rate: Korean Won/US Dollar. *Source* Statistics Korea (http://kosis.kr)

enhancing transparency in corporate management. In November 2000, 29 firms were liquidated. Major companies such as LG Semi-conductor and Daewoo were forced to engage more actively in M&A, combined financial sheets were enforced, and firms had to lower their debt ratio. Consequently, many of the M&A regulations were abolished, transparency of corporate accounting was enhanced, and firm performance was improved.

The labor market reform aimed to increase flexibility in the labor market along with improving labor conditions. The Korea Tripartite was established in January

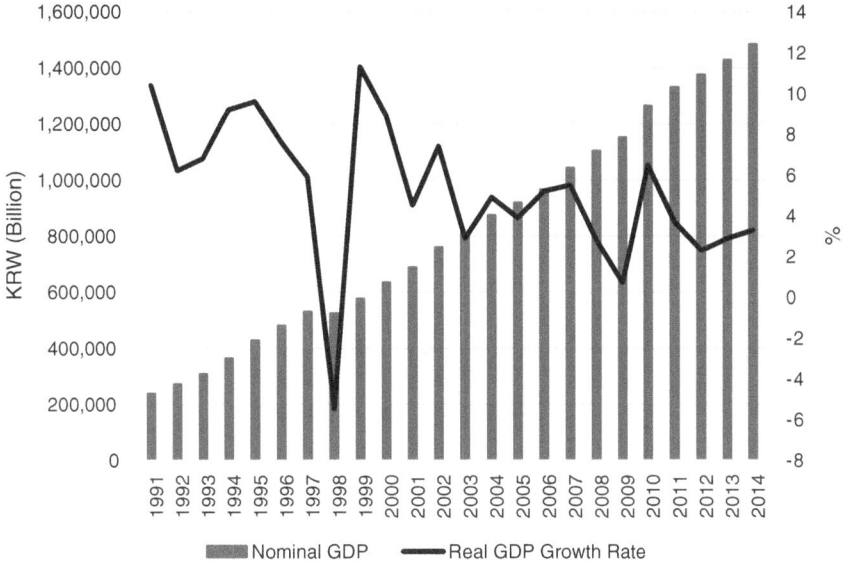

Fig. 2.3 Real GDP growth rate. *Source* Statistics Korea (http://kosis.kr)

1998 to discuss labor policy and build consensus among stakeholders, while the Korean Confederation of Trade Unions was legalized. Coverage of the Labor Standard Act, Minimum Wages Act, and labor insurance was expanded to enhance the protection of workers. At the same time, the employment adjustment and dispatch of workers system was enacted in 1998 to increase labor market flexibility.

Finally, the public sector reform focused on the state bureaucracy from the neo-liberal perspective to remove the privilege of career bureaucrats in their job security and decision-making power, and to improve efficiency of public administration by privatizing policy functions which had been under bureaucrat control. For example, in the public sector, new public management reforms such as agencification, marketization, performance appraisal and performance-based rewards as well as open rank recruitment have been adopted.

2.3   Changes in the Policy Environment

2.3.1   Political Change

2.3.1.1   Legislative Power and Divided Government

Enhanced democracy and political freedom is the key political change after the historical juncture of the 6/29 declaration. This political change implies that politics, not national planning, became central in setting state goals in terms of both

Table 2.1 The majority party in the legislature

Year	General election	Majority party	Seats	Proportion (%)
1985–1988	12th	Democratic Justice Party	148	53.6
1988–1992	13th	Democratic Justice Party	125	41.8
1992–1996	14th	Democratic Liberal Party	149	49.8
1996–2000	15th	*New Korea Party*	139	46.5
2000–2004	16th	*Grand National Party*	133	48.7
2004–2008	17th	Uri Party	152	50.8
2008–2012	18th	Grand National Party	153	51.2
2012–2016	19th	Saenuri Party	152	50.7
2016–2020	20th	*Minjoo Party of Korea*	123	41

Note Italics indicate opponent party
Source Korean National Assembly (http://www.assembly.go.kr)

substance and process. The increased awareness of the importance of social welfare and equity after the 6/29 declaration illustrates a consequence of the change in that the demand for social welfare and equity had been suppressed during the developmental era. This is a significant deviation from the traditional policy direction, considering that South Korea had been a typical developmental state until then.

Another significant change in the policy environment is the strengthened and extended legislative power. First, tools for checks and balances of power were restored in the new Constitution, such as the authority of the National Assembly to investigate the administration every year as well as when necessary, and to ratify major domestic and foreign policies. Second, this constitutional revision was accompanied by a changing political landscape. A divided government became the norm rather than the exception; the legislature, including the local assemblies, has often been dominated by the opponent parties. As shown in Table 2.1, in many election terms the government has either been divided or the ruling party failed to occupy half of the seats in the National Assembly. Combined with the constitutional revision, this divided government setting significantly constrained presidential power and strengthened legislative power.

2.3.1.2 Crisis of Representative Democracy

Although the political changes have opened up opportunities for the legislature to take initiative in policy decision making, scholars lament the crisis of party politics and representative democracy in South Korea (Choi 2002; Kim 2014). The sources of the crisis are manifold. First, the level of trust in the legislature is the lowest among public institutions, which has triggered a vicious cycle of low performance and low trust in turn. Second, popular politics that resort directly to the public have increased. Democratization in South Korea, instead of depending on representative democracy, was partly achieved through anti-government movements led by two popular political celebrities, Kim Young-sam and Kim Dae-jung. Further, citizens considered such 'outside' politicians as Roh Moo-hyun and Ahn Cheol Soo more reliable and honest than politicians within representative institutions. Outside politicians also responded eagerly to the public directly. Third, an increased number of elections and citizen swing votes made the legislative branch respond more sensitively to mass opinion. Frequent elections at the national and local level are by no means a problem in a democracy; however, in the absence of a decentralized party structure, every election is eventually managed and interpreted as a national, winner-take-all game, leaving little buffer for pluralistic politics. Finally, an increase in the desire for direct citizen participation in policy decision making has also affected the legitimacy of the legislature. There is a struggle in South Korean politics to find a balance between representative and participatory democracy.

2.3.2 Social Change

2.3.2.1 Rise of the Pluralistic Civil Society

Political democratization after 1987 was made possible by the rise of civil society during the developmental era, and pushed civil society to flourish even further. The establishment and collapse of the Fourth Republic is often understood as showing the eroded foundation of the authoritarian regime and the growth of civil society that was brought by the economic success of the very same regime (Choi 2002). The diversity of interests and values among civil society began to find institutional venues through which to be expressed and realized. For example, Fig. 2.4 shows an impressive increase in the number of labor unions and their membership during the late 1980s, a decrease during the 1990s, and a stabilization after the financial crisis.

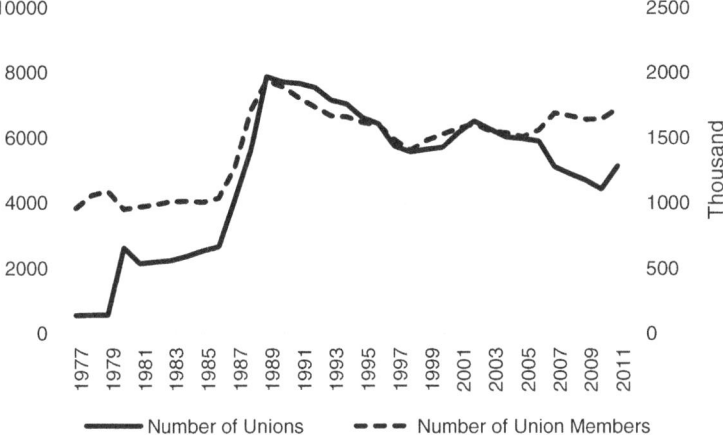

Fig. 2.4 Membership increase in labor unions. *Source* Statistics Korea (http://kosis.kr)

One of the major characteristics of the Korean developmental state was a nation-wide corporatism structure, with one state-authorized peak organization per sector. For example, in the education sector, only the Korean Federation of Teachers' Associations (KFTA) was authorized to represent the interests of the sector. Likewise, the Federation of Korean Trade Unions (FKTU) was the only authorized partner of the government in the area of labor policy (Jung 2014: 29). After the 6/29 declaration, however, there was an explosion of civic organizations including workers' organizations, farmers' organizations, and civil rights organizations. This increased diversity also changed the state corporatism structure (Jung 2014: 29). In the education sector, the Korean Teachers and Education Workers Union was established in 1989, co-existing with the KFTA. In the labor sector, the Korean Confederation of Trade Unions was established in 1995, which had already been seeded in 1987, competing with the existing FKTU. These multiple representations of peak organizations in various sectors made the policy environment even more complex.

2.3.2.2 Increased Social Instability

The increase in labor market flexibility and the number of non-regular workers, which we will discuss later in this section, imply a gradual collapse of the middle class which should theoretically provide a high level of support for democracy. Although there is still debate on the current status of the middle class in South Korea, there are signs that the middle class is in serious danger in terms of numbers and prospects. In the 1980s, 60–80% of citizens responded that they belonged to the middle class (Kang et al. 2014). In 2006, according to Statistics Korea, only 53% of the respondents claimed to belong to the middle class. In 2012, according to the Hyundai Research Institute, only 46% of respondents thought they belonged to the middle class. This is a noticeable warning to Korean society, as the collapse of the middle class often leads to the polarization of society and a crisis of democracy.

As firms have reduced organization size and employment, many people have accepted decreased salaries or lost their jobs in the absence of a social safety net provided by the government. Some social symptoms are by no means positive. For example, the suicide rate can be an indicator of the level of social health. Figure 2.5 shows the relatively high and increasing suicide rate in South Korea compared to other OECD countries. It shows that the suicide rate in South Korea has been soaring since the 2000s. The suicide rate among the older generation who are socially and economically isolated is even higher: during the late 2000s, the suicide rates for people in their 70s and 80s were around 80 and 120 per 100,000 citizens, respectively (Fig. 2.6).

Finally, the most fundamental change that would define the social policy environment is the problem of an aging society. The population in South Korea is aging so fast that the increase in household income cannot protect the old generation from falling into financial risk. In addition, the birth rate fell below 2.0 in the 1990s and

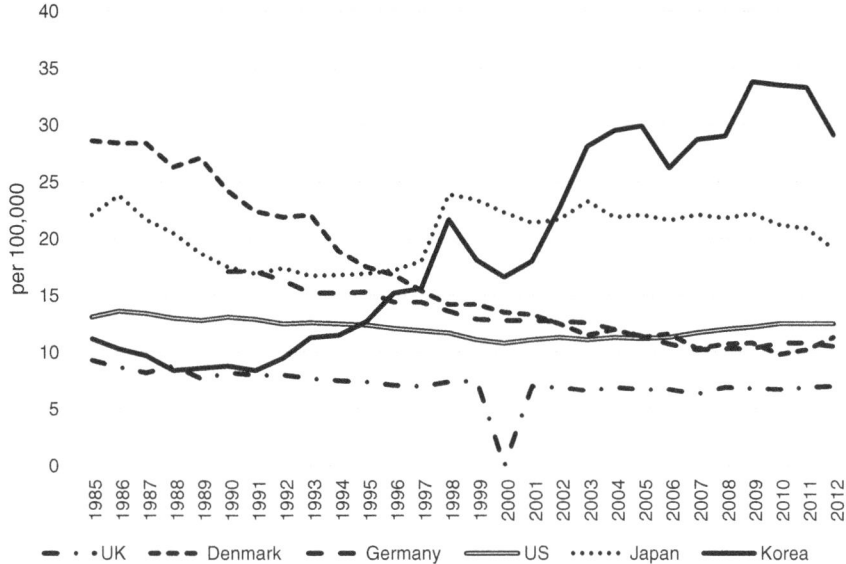

Fig. 2.5 Suicide rate: OECD countries and South Korea. *Source* OECD Health Data (http://data. oecd.org)

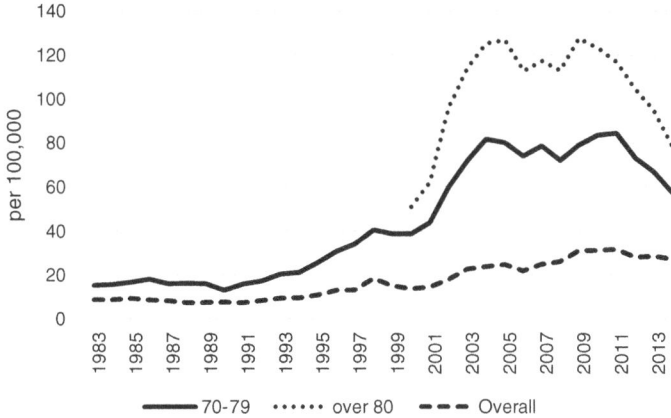

Fig. 2.6 Suicide rate in South Korea by age. *Source* Statistics Korea (http://kosis.kr)

has remained around 1.2 since the 2000s (Statistics Korea). With insufficient social safety and low quality of life, it is not likely that the birth rate will recover to a sustainable level.

Overall, these symptoms demonstrate significant social changes in the policy environment in South Korea. The collapse of the middle class and the polarization of the distribution of economic opportunities across society could inhibit social consensus building and policy decision making. Korean society seems to suffer from a low level of psychological safety, life satisfaction, and social trust, all of which could create major policy challenges in the near future.

2.3.3   Economic Change

2.3.3.1   Globalization and Global Standards

Although scholars usually identify South Korea as a developmental state or typify its production regime as a coordinated market economy based on authoritarian political structure (Evans 1995; Hall and Soskice 2001; Kim 2014; Soskice 1999), it is interesting that the administrations have long been trying to transform its production regime to look more like a free market economy. Even before the financial crisis, the Korean economy had been incrementally exposed to the global economy in the process of globalization. The establishment of the World Trade Organization in 1995 constrained the available government policy tools. The Uruguay Round (1986–1994) marked the end of the favorable global trade environment, which had been one of the key conditions for the Korean developmental state to succeed. Admission to the Organization for Economic Co-operation and Development (OECD) in 1996 was another significant change that further limited the policy leverage useful for the government to control the financial market and domestic industry. South Korea entered a new era with different environmental challenges. Scholars often argue that one of the major causes of the Korean financial crisis is that the financial market became open to global hedge funds that make the national financial market unstable in the short term (Lim and Jang 2006).

The reforms pushed by the Kim Dae-jung administration after the financial crisis were intended to contribute to meeting the neo-liberal requirements of global creditors including the IMF. Accordingly, actors in the private sector in South Korea were required to accept global standards.[5] For example, firms had to apply the global accounting system and pursue ISO certification to compete in the global market.

2.3.3.2   Labor Market Flexibility

The reforms of the Kim Dae-jung administration focused on the renewal of the national economic system through setting global standards in the financial market, corporate governance, the labor market, and the public sector to achieve global

---

[5]It should be noted that the financial crisis not only drove economic globalization but also social globalization. As Rosendorf (2000) claimed that globalization is ultimately a social and cultural phenomenon, globalization was a process of global standardization and isomorphism.

Table 2.2 Gap in the length of service between full-time and non-regular workers in 2014

	Average	Shorter than 1 year (%)	1–3 years (%)	Longer than 3 years (%)	Total (%)
Total	5 years 7 months	32.3	21.5	46.1	100
Full-time	7 years 1 month	21.6	21.7	56.7	100
Non-regular	2 years 6 months	54.8	21.1	24.1	100

Source Statistics Korea (http://kosis.kr)

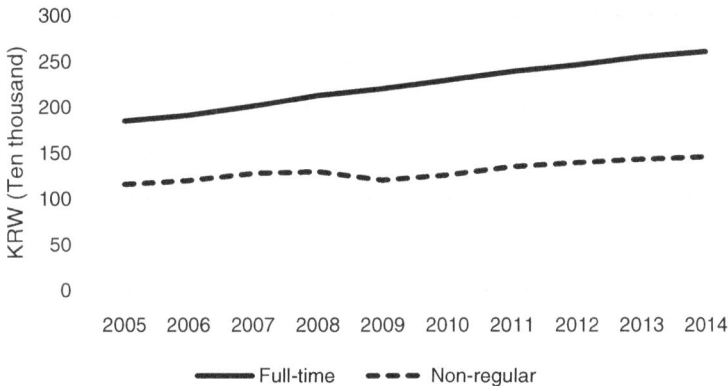

Fig. 2.7 Monthly wage gap between full-time and non-regular workers. *Source* Statistics Korea (http://kosis.kr)

competitiveness. In the global market in the absence of protective trade policies, labor productivity was the key to maintaining competitiveness. To compensate for low labor productivity, firms increased labor intensity on the one hand and the government increased the flexibility of labor contracts on the other hand. According to the Statistics Korea, the ratio of non-regular workers went up during the early 2000s, and remained stable at around 30–40%, while the average ratio of non-regular workers across OECD countries was 11.4% in 2015.[6] Table 2.2 demonstrates the gap between full-time and non-regular workers in their length of service. While the average length of service of full-time workers was 7 years and 1 month in 2014, that of non-regular workers was only 2 years and 6 months. While 56.7% of full-time workers remained in the same job for more than 3 years, 54.8% of non-regular workers stayed in the same job for less than 1 year. Continuous labor market reforms and increased labor market flexibility resulted in an increased wage gap between full-time and non-regular workers. In 2005 the average wage of non-regular workers was about 63% of that of full-time workers; in 2014, the ratio dropped to 56% (Fig. 2.7).

---

[6]http://stats.oecd.org/Index.aspx?DataSetCode=TEMP_I.

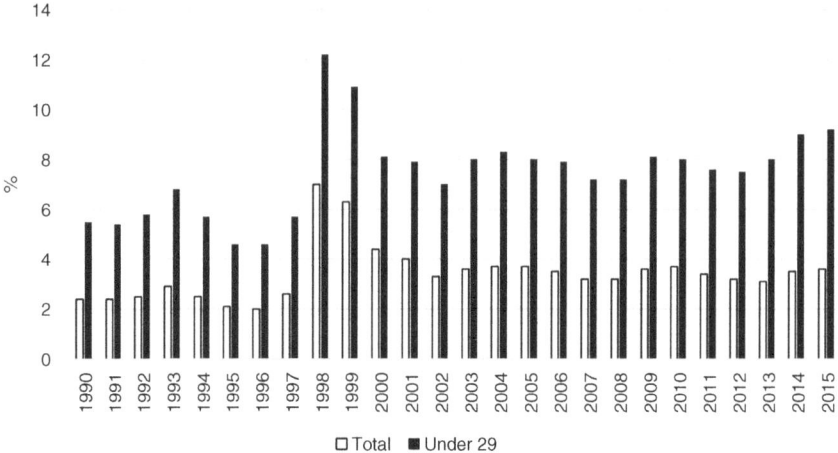

Fig. 2.8 Unemployment rate: total and under the age of 29. *Source* Statistics Korea (http://kosis.kr)

The increase in labor market flexibility, when combined with low economic performance, negatively affected the quality of employment. Neither the number of unemployed people nor the unemployment rate increased much after the financial crisis. What is remarkable is the difference between the total unemployment rate and that of the younger generation as shown in Fig. 2.8. The unemployment rate for those under the age of 29 has at times been more than twice the total unemployment rate. Low economic performance along with labor market flexibility seems to have affected the younger generation more severely.

Overall, in terms of economic changes, the Korean state was no longer able to design and implement state-driven economic policies as the national economy became globally and substantively open and complex. Bureaucratic or developmental planning yielded its position as the primary governance mechanism to the market mechanism. At the same time, the state failed to provide a sufficient social safety net to protect workers and citizens at risk. The Korean state is still in transition in terms of its production regime, but the transition does not seem to have resulted in improved performance.

2.4 Challenges to Key Policy Actors

Changes in the organizational environment mean challenges to the organizations dwelling in the environment. The political, social, and economic changes discussed above ask for adaptive responses from public institutions including the president (and the presidential office), legislature, and state bureaucracy. At the same time, in turn, these actors also contribute to the changes of their policy environment, as we saw in such a political event as the 6/29 declaration.

In this section we analyze challenges that were brought by the changes in the policy environment to key policy actors: presidents, legislature, and state bureaucracy. Particularly, we focus on the institutional disparity caused by the two major events of the 6/29 declaration and the financial crisis, and on the mutual influence among presidents, legislature, and state bureaucracy driven by their respective responses to the changing environment.

2.4.1 The Presidency

To discuss challenges that were brought by the changes in the policy environment to presidents, it is first necessary to understand how the political context of the policy environment weaved the state institutions around the presidency. Scholars characterize the institutional arrangement of the period that endowed presidents with dominant power as a so-called imperial presidency.[7] We can summarize the conditions that led to the imperial presidency in South Korea as follows.

First, the weak legislative branch was the key. Under the representative democracy system, the president shares political legitimacy with the legislature. The imperial presidency in South Korea was possible when the legislative branch failed to assume political legitimacy and the political parties were captured by the presidents' agenda.[8] Second, the political ideology that emphasized national security and economic development justified the concentration of power and government-driven rather than citizen-driven policy. Third, the political culture has been based on patriarchal authority and collectivism, in which the culturally acceptable alternative to reducing coordination costs has been centralized public administration and ultimate coordination by the president. The authoritarian presidency, perceived as reducing coordination costs, ensured a certain degree of political legitimacy. Finally, the long-term seizure of power by one person solidified all these conditions. In the absence of competing elites and their periodical change, democratic control was simply impossible (Schumpeter 1943).

These institutional conditions that supported the imperial presidency, however, have been gradually eroded for the last thirty years. The condition of a weak legislative branch has changed enormously. Scholars often highlight the power shift from the president to the National Assembly (Choi 2002; Kim 2014). As we have seen in Table 2.1, in many legislative terms after the 6/29 declaration, presidents suffered from divided governments, which made it difficult to pass bills they initiated. Even under the condition of a unified government, the president had to face

---

[7]The origin of the term imperial presidency is not clear (Choi 2002). At the least, we need to distinguish its meaning when the term is used in the United States and South Korea. In the former, it usually refers to the president's exclusive power with regard to foreign policy. In the latter, it usually refers to the president's unconstrained power in both domestic and foreign affairs (Choi 2002), mainly emphasizing the president's control over the legislature and the court.

[8]Until the 2000s, the presidents were also the chief of the ruling party.

stronger political voices from the opponent parties and weaker political support from the ruling party.[9] Moreover, since the single-term system with direct election was adopted after the 6/29 declaration, every president has become a political lame duck at the end of the term. The policy initiatives, especially reform agendas, were not implemented effectively as the presidential term approached the fourth or the final year. Long-term seizure of power no longer exists as an institutional condition. As a result, although the president is still the most powerful actor in the state, the status has changed from monopolistic decision maker to one of the powerful actors in the policy process.

The social changes discussed above required a president to consider more political agendas than economic development; democracy, social equity, political freedom, and a smaller government were called for by civil society. The critical challenge for the president after the 6/29 declaration and the financial crisis is the increased demand to meet both goals. Basically, the coordinated market economy system or the developmental state was institutionally revised to a significant degree as a result of the 6/29 declaration and the Kim Dae-jung administration reforms, resulting in the state losing coordination capacity. However, the production regime did not change to a liberal one but rather to a hybrid form, the performance of which is not proven yet. Accordingly, trust in the president has remained lower than in the period of economic development. Traditional forms of mass media, which obtained autonomy from the government through the abolition of the Basic Press Act in 1987, were prone to criticizing the president and the government. The rise of new social media, which is usually used by civic movement groups, also negatively affects trust in the president.

2.4.2 The Legislature

When we turn our attention to the legislature, we already discussed the crisis of representative democracy that reflects a bipolarization of political ideology in society (Kim 2014). The neo-liberal reforms following the financial crisis in South Korea in 1997 were on a wider global stream, and it is not surprising that Korean society has experienced similar polarization like other developing countries under a financial crisis.[10] This social ideological polarization, combined with majority rule, resulted in political deadlock in the National Assembly. Although the institutional and legal authority of the legislature was expanded in the current Constitution, the

---

[9]Revisions and delay of bills occurred frequently, as shown in the Labor Reform Act by the Kim Young-sam administration in 1996 and procrastinated reforms during the Kim Dae-jung administration due to *chaebol* resistance.

[10]Even the United States has been warned against increasingly polarization (Pew Research Center 2014).

original function of the legislature, which is the authoritative distribution of values and coordination of social conflicts, does not work well enough to earn citizen trust.

First, the top-down manner of candidate nomination in a political party, in spite of long-time efforts to reform it, still works in practice. The top-down candidate nomination for general and local elections reflects the ongoing influence of the core members of the party such as the president and party leaders. The centralization of power within the parties results in bipolarized politics, which in turn reflects and strengthens bipolarized society and public opinion. A simplified diagnosis of social problems and solutions leaves no room for collaboration; in the long term, therefore, what we observe is "angry constituents." The angry constituents put pressure on the parties to show exclusive loyalty to their own constituents by keeping their position firm rather than muddling through compromise, even by sacrificing the potential benefits both sides would receive if consensus could eventually be reached.

Another issue within the legislature is the revised articles of the National Assembly Act from 2012. The Act strictly limited the authority of the National Assembly Chairman to discretionally postulate a bill. To pass a bill "rapidly," which practically means to pass a bill by the ruling party alone, 60% of the members of the National Assembly must agree. The concept of the filibuster was also introduced. Although these new articles were intended to enhance democracy by preventing the passage of bills by the ruling party without the agreement of the opponent parties, they are sometimes argued to break the principle of the majority rule and delay the legislation process.

2.4.3 State Bureaucracy

Scholars have pointed out diverse factors for the rapid development in the Korean economy during the 1970s and 1980s. These include strong presidential leadership, citizen desire for education which has led to high-quality labor supply, and favorable global trade environments (Jung 2014; Woo-Cumings 1999). State theorists particularly emphasized the role of state bureaucrats who are mostly career bureaucrats rather than politically appointed ones (Johnson 1982). State bureaucrats have played a pivotal role in the economic development of South Korea. Not only did they devote themselves to implementing economic policies decided by the presidents, but they were also endowed with decision power for major economic policies during the Park Chung-hee and Chun Doo-hwan administrations.

During the developmental era, state bureaucrats were among the best human capital in the country. In the absence of attractive jobs in the private sector, many of the best young students in South Korea pursued work in the public sector by passing the competitive national exam, resulting in the enhancement of overall state capability. This elite group typical in developmental states enjoyed the support and protection of the president. Being politically immune to the influence of the

National Assembly and interest groups, state bureaucrats in the pilot agencies planned and implemented state-driven economic growth policies under the presidents' strong leadership.

The "success story" of the Korean state bureaucracy began to crack after the 6/29 declaration and the financial crisis. As discussed above, democratization since the 6/29 declaration has weakened presidential power in the policy process. First of all, as the presidential term was set to five years with no consecutive terms of service, environmental uncertainty from a bureaucrat viewpoint has increased. Since the 6/29 declaration, South Korea has experienced two peaceful political turnovers, which accompanied comprehensive policy changes from the political right to left, and vice versa. Second, the state bureaucracy can no longer enjoy the support and protection of the president as it did before; it is now more exposed to and controlled by the legislature, strong interest groups, and mass media. The political checks by the legislature have been institutionalized; strong interest groups argue for their interests more actively by utilizing different avenues of political participation including petition, negotiation, and even collective action. As a result, the policy process has become much more complex; frequent symptoms of state bureaucrats losing their policy initiative include complication of related policies, delay of policy implementation, and decrease in policy consistency.

The financial crisis in 1997 pushed the challenges for the state bureaucracy even further. The key negative impact of the financial crisis on the state bureaucracy is the erosion of public trust in the ability and ethics of career bureaucrats. They were criticized as having failed to prevent the financial crisis and buckling under pressure from the IMF. The image of the state bureaucracy fell from able and efficient hero of national and economic development to the "villain of the piece" in terms of the financial crisis and following policy failures. It is not surprising that the Kim Dae-jung administration took a comprehensive approach to reforming the public sector, as we discussed in the previous section.

2.4.4   Summary

We can summarize the challenges for key policy actors as follows. First, as the political ideology has changed from national security and economic development to democracy, social equity, and welfare, the political culture that sustained the authoritarian system or the imperial presidency has changed from patriarchal authoritarianism and collectivism to political freedom of individuals and private interests. Second, after the 6/29 declaration, the expanded civic movement created interest group politics within Korean politics, resulting in a strengthened role played by the legislature. Third, the financial crisis significantly damaged citizen trust in the government, particularly the ability of the state bureaucracy.

As a result of these influences from outside, the relationship between the president and the legislature has changed. Presidents often become political lame ducks, combined with decreased support from the ruling party and increased political resistance from the opponent parties, as well as the increased possibility of a divided government and a shorter presidential term. The legislature, however, does not seem to fully utilize this opportunity, partly due to its institutional limitations such as the top-down candidate nomination system of major political parties, the revised National Assembly Act, an insufficient level of expertise, and stronger influence from interest groups.

Finally, the state bureaucracy does not seem to aptly respond to the change in political ideology and culture. It needs to achieve a shift in organizational goals from economic development to social welfare and deregulation, which require different organizational capacity from planning and control. Political culture does not sustain the values of bureaucracy. The relationship to the legislature is on a path away from a developmental state toward a representative democracy. The relationship with the president is more complex than before; although the state bureaucracy still remains as an institutional servant of the president, it is possible that the ties could be weakened as the state bureaucracy is now more fragmented, hollowed out, and open to outside influence.

2.5 Conclusion

In this chapter, we described the environmental changes in public policy in South Korea after the 1980s. We focused on the political, social, and economic environment of public policy, and identified the 6/29 declaration in 1987 and the financial crisis in 1997 as two major critical junctures in the process of the institutionalization of the contemporary Korean state. While the former heavily influenced the political path to democracy, the latter influenced not only the economic system but also the whole social system of South Korea. The influence of the financial crisis still remains while politicians realize the shortcomings of the 1987 Constitution for further democracy and social integration.

The establishment of the 1987 Constitution strengthened basic civil rights and the power of the legislature while weakening the presidential power. The restoration of democracy in South Korea after 1987 was impressive as there were two periods of peaceful political turnover in 1998 and 2008 (Huntington 1993). Liberal democracy, social equity, and welfare were put at the center of political ideology. Interest group politics have been facilitated and reflected in the policy process as labor unions, farmer associations, and anti-government intellectuals advocated the interests of minority groups that did not equitably benefit from economic growth.

Although these changes in the policy environment contributed to the democratization of the policy decision-making process, they have also incurred confusion in public decision making. From the institutional disparities that occurred in the transition from a coordinated market economy to a hybrid one, Korean society is witnessing an increase in coordination costs that include a burst of the pursuit of private interest without social responsibility at the social level, and corruption as well as lack of accountability at the bureaucracy level. The state bureaucracy, which has been a loyal servant of the president, is now increasingly fragmented and co-opted by strong interest groups, resulting in bureaucratic clientelism.

What direction will the Korean state take? Authoritarian solutions that are based on suppressive governmental authority are no longer politically viable. The authority and capacity of the government have not been proportionally increased to the degree of conflict among different interest groups. At the same time, however, a completely free market economy is also not viable; South Korea simply does not have historical experience in running that kind of social and economic system. The Korean state is in the middle of two ideal production regimes: coordinated and free market economy (Allen 2004; Soskice 1999). It is most plausible that the new state institutionalization could head for a variation of the coordinated market economy, but has not established its own regime that ensures institutional coherence. For the Korean state to complete its transition from an authoritarian to a democratic and liberal system, a balance between reforms of formal institutions and long-term changes in informal institutions such as social values, political ideology and culture, citizen attitudes, and ethics is warranted.

References

Alavi H (1979) The state in post-colonial societies: Pakistan and Bangladesh. In: Goubourne H (ed) Politics and state in the third world. Macmillan, London

Allen M (2004) The varieties of capitalism paradigm: not enough variety? Socio-Econ Rev 2: 87–108

Bedeski RE (1994) The transformation of South Korea: reform and reconstruction in the sixth republic under Roh Tae-woo, 1987–1992. Routledge, New York

Choi J (2002) Democracy after democratization: the Korean experience. Humanitas, Seoul

Evans P (1995) Embedded autonomy: states and industrial transformation. Princeton University Press, Princeton

Hall P, Soskice D (eds) (2001) Varieties of capitalism: the institutional foundations of comparative advantage. Oxford University Press, Oxford

Heo U, Roehrig T (2010) South Korea since 1980. Cambridge University Press, New York

Huntington SP (1993) The third wave: democratization in the late twentieth century, vol 4. University of Oklahoma Press, Okalahoma

Ji J (2011) The origin and formation of neoliberalization of South Korea. Bookworld, Seoul

Johnson C (1982) MITI and the Japanese miracle: the growth of industrial policy: 1925–1975. Stanford University Press, Stanford

Jung Y (2014) The Korean State, public administration, and development: past, present, and future challenges. Seoul National University Press, Seoul

Kang W, Kim B, Ahn S, Yee J, Choi I (2014) Are you in the middle class: anatomy of social class conflicts. 21st Century Books, Seoul

Kim S (2014) Korean democratization and the asian financial crisis: toward normalizing representative democracy. In: Lee TJ et al (eds) Transformation of Korean society after the foreign currency crisis: changes in politics, economy, and welfare. Hanul Books, Seoul, pp 66–131

Lim H, Jang J (2006) Neo-Liberalism in post-crisis South Korea: social conditions and outcomes. J Contemp Asia 36(4):442–463

Pew Research Center (2014) Political polarization in the American public

Robertson PJ, Choi T (2010) Ecological governance: organizing principles for an emerging era. Publ Adm Rev 70(1):89–99

Rosendorf NM (2000) Social and cultural globalization: concepts, history, and America's role. In: Nye JS, Donahue JD (eds) Governance in a globalizing world. Brookings Institute, Washington, D.C., pp 109–134

Schumpeter JA (1943) Capitalism in the postwar world

Soskice D (1999) Divergent production regimes: coordinated and uncoordinated market economies in the 1980s and 1990s. In: Kitschelt H, Lange P, Marks G, Stephens JD (eds) Continuity and change in contemporary capitalism. Cambridge University Press, Cambridge, pp 101–134

Weiss L (1998) The myth of the powerless state. Cornell University Press, Ithaca

Woo-Cumings M (1999) The development state. Cornell University Press, Ithaca

Chapter 3
Leaving Behind the Developmental State: The Changing Rationale of Governance in Korean Governments

Huck-ju Kwon

3.1 Introduction

This chapter examines the rationale of governance in Korean governments over the past twenty years after democratization, and try to answer the question as to whether Korean governments have come up with a new rationale of governance different from that of the developmental state. There has been a large body of literature on the developmental state regarding the Korean government, which examines the relationship between the state and society (Haggard 1994; Kim and Vogel 2011; Woo-Cumings 1999). The previous volume of *Korean Government and Public Policy* also looks into the inner workings of the government, including the ways in which the developmental state has organized government agencies and implemented public policies in the period of rapid economic development (Kwon and Koo 2014). We have also witnessed a renewed interest in the developmental state from scholars of developmental studies who are keen to elicit policy lessons for other developing countries (Mkandawire 2001). Nevertheless, the Korean governments over the past twenty years have tried to move beyond the developmental state. There has been a widely shared contention that Korea needs a new idea of governance in order to move beyond authoritarian politics and consolidate economic development. There is, however, little research into changes in the rationale of governance in the Korean governments after democratization: Does the idea of the developmental state still provide a relevant rationale for governments after democratization? Or has a new rationale of governance come about?

Although the developmental state was very successful in the area of economic development, it was regarded as a historic legacy of the authoritarian government and could therefore not be an effective rationale for democratic governance to tackle policy challenges of the future. It was something to be left behind. Past governments

H. Kwon (✉)
Graduate School of Public Administration, Seoul National University, Seoul, South Korea
e-mail: hkwon4@snu.ac.kr

© Springer International Publishing AG 2017
J. Choi et al. (eds.), *The Korean Government and Public Policies in a Development Nexus*, The Political Economy of the Asia Pacific,
DOI 10.1007/978-3-319-52473-3_3

such as the Kim Young-sam government explicitly announced that they would discard the idea of a state-centered policy regime like that of the developmental state. Other governments such as under Roh Moo-hyun tried to put different methods of public sector management into practice. This chapter examines the policy efforts of the Korean governments under Kim Young-sam, Kim Dae-jung, Roh Moo-hyun, and Lee Myung-bak to ascertain whether they came up with a coherent and consistent paradigm to govern the country.

3.2   The Rationale of Governance and the Developmental State

We refer to governance as purposeful activities by public actors and institutions to achieve public goals. The rationale of governance is to provide a certain theoretical direction to organize policy processes in order to achieve those policy goals. As Lane separates public policy processes into the three main components of policy goals, instruments and policy actors (Lane 1987), the rationale of governance will guide policy actors on how to choose and utilize policy instruments in order to achieve those goals.

The rationale of governance also defines the ways in which government agencies work together with other policy actors to achieve policy goals. Further, it guides the overall relationship between the state and social and economic actors. It is essential for a government to have a coherent rationale of governance which helps navigate through social and economic challenges that arise in domestic and global settings. When Hall discusses policy paradigm (Hall 1993), he also emphasizes these three dimensions for capturing the rationale of policy paradigm: first, the goal of public policy; second, the role of the state in relation to society and economy; and third, the policy instruments to be applied to achieve those goals. These three dimensions are applied in this chapter in order to analyze the rationale of governance over the past two decades.

It is not true that every government has a clear and coherent rationale of governance. When a new government comes to office, it often claims that it has a new rationale of governance. This does not necessarily mean that the new government actually has a theoretically coherent and consistent rationale of governance. The head of the government, the President or the Prime Minister, may only give the public political rhetoric about policy goals and approaches. In contrast, some governments such as the Margaret Thatcher government came to office with a coherent paradigm of governance which had a long gestation period beforehand. Her government set out a different relationship between the government and other social actors such as trade unions, and introduced new policy innovations such as the privatization of public utilities.

How do we know whether a government has a coherent rationale of governance? Hall used an approach to trace ideational trajectories with a focus on the three dimensions discussed above (Hall 1993). It is a very useful approach when the government under study has a well-articulated rationale of governance. It would, however, be difficult to reconstruct it in the case that the government under focus may not have an elaborated rationale. In order to deal with this problem, we will first contrast the governance rationale of the government in question with the previous one, and discuss to what extent there are differences. In this chapter, we will further discuss the rationale of governance in Korean governments in relation to that of the developmental state.

For such a purpose it is necessary to first discuss the developmental state as a rationale of governance according to three dimensions. Although the notion of the developmental state was first put forward in order to explain economic development in Japan (Johnson 1982), it captures well the rationale of governance of the Korean government under President Park Chung-hee. He took power through a military coup d'état on 16 May 1961 and embarked on an ambitious economic development plan, which proved to be very successful. The authoritarian government adopted a state-led development strategy with first import-substitute and later export-oriented industrialization. Economic growth was the foremost goal for the Korean government under Park Chung-hee (Woo 1991). Other social values such as equality and social rights were relegated to secondary consideration. For instance, social policy programs for the poor and disabled were never placed high on the government agenda (Kwon 1999). Park made it very clear in his words (Park 1963: 177):

> I want to emphasize and reemphasize that the key factor of the May 16 revolution was in effect an industrial revolution. ...My chief concern, however, was economic revolution.

In terms of state and society relations, the Korean government under Park Chung-hee enjoyed large space for autonomy in relation to social classes. Since Korea was a mainly agricultural society where the majority of people worked in the agricultural sector, the landowning class might have put the state under political constraints from pursuing policies which would undermine their economic and political interest. In reality, the landowning class was disintegrated by the land reform which was undertaken in the wake of liberation in 1945. Other social classes such as the working class had not yet emerged by the early 1960s before Korea embarked on industrialization efforts.

With strong support from President Park, the Economic Planning Board was able to steer different government ministries to work together for the overall goal of economic development (Choi 2014). The Economic Planning Board played a role as a pilot agency which developed the five-year economic plan and coordinated competing ministries. It also convened regular national conferences under the auspice of President Park for different policy actors including bureaucrats from the local governments, farmers in rural areas, small business owners and their workers. The government was also able to mobilize economic efforts to increase industrial output and export (Amsden 1989). Government controlled banks proved to be very useful instruments to induce private business to maximize their economic performance through credit and favored interest rates.

The dark side of the developmental state was political oppression and economic exclusion. President Park changed the Constitution a couple of times in order to continue his rule. In 1971, the so-called Yushin Constitution effectively allowed him to be President for life and the National Assembly became a rubber-stamp institution with one-third of its members appointed by the President. Political protest was harshly oppressed and many political campaigners for democracy were put into prison. Trade unions were not allowed, so workers demanding wage increases were practically ignored. Such political oppression and economic exclusion was justified under the pretext of economic development and communist threat of North Korea. It also raises a difficult question to answer: Is the authoritarian government with a heavy hand for political oppression and economic exclusion a necessary condition for the developmental state? Or is it possible to deploy the policy regime of the developmental state without resorting to authoritarian politics? White floated the idea of the democratic developmental state which is able to mobilize policy efforts for economic development while maintaining a democratic political process (White 1998). However, there is still a clear divide among academic and political commentators about the inseparability of the developmental state and authoritarian politics.

3.3   The 'Civilian' Government and Market Liberalization

After the collapse of the democratically elected government in 1961 through the military coup d'état, Kim Young-sam was the first elected President in three decades with a civilian background. His predecessor, Roh Tae-woo who was elected by popular vote, participated in the military coup d'état organized by Chun Doo-hwan with other generals. Kim called his government the 'Civilian Government' to distinguish it from the previous governments. He was determined to sever the legacy of the previous authoritarian governments by banning informal political cliques in the army which were a nurturing ground for politically ambitious generals. He also brought charges against two former military Presidents for corruption and treason who were sentenced to life-time imprisonment. It was a bold move to sever the political legacy of the military government.

In the area of economic reform, President Kim carried out equally sweeping actions. In order to prevent corruption among politicians and bureaucrats, his government first introduced new regulations on banking transactions. Under the regulations, all persons and businesses were required to do their banking with their real names and subject to strict identity checks. Previously, people could conduct banking transactions with false names and banks did not check a person's identity. Because of this, the informal economy was very large and money laundering was very easy. After the new banking regulations, banking transactions could be traced by the authorities once the court issued a warrant. The Kim government also introduced a measure that would force senior government officials to declare their assets every year so that the public could find out about changes in their wealth. It was an effort to clean up the government bureaucracy, and many senior politicians and bureaucrats were dismissed for corruption.

The Kim government also banned the registration of property assets under someone else's name. The ban of trustee assets was also part of anti-corruption and tax-evasion efforts. It was a widespread practice to register one's own assets under someone else's name. This was done for many purposes such as hiding one's property assets, carrying out illegal transactions or evading high taxes. These new regulations on property registration not only prohibited such ill-intended transactions, but also established an institutional infrastructure for transparent and trustworthy market activities. It is also worth mentioning that the Korean government was able to enforce such regulations very effectively using information technology set up for the government and banking sector.

The Kim government also made it clear that it would carry out public sector reforms that would reduce the scope of government and policy interventions. The government should leave private initiatives to set the market orientation instead of state-led policy intervention for economic development. The Public Administration Reform Commission was set up in 1993 in order to reduce government regulations that had hindered private economic initiatives. The Public Administration Reform Commission was able to reduce about 6000 regulations (Public Admiration Reform Commission 1994).

The number of government ministries and civil servants of the central government was also reduced. Nine positions for ministers and deputy ministers were abolished and the positions of about 1100 civil servants in the central government were reduced. The Ministry of Commerce and Industries and the Ministry of Energy and Resource were merged into the Ministry of Trade and Industries while the Ministry of Postal Affairs was changed to the Ministry of Information and Communications. The most notable reorganization of the government ministries was to merge the Ministry of Economic Planning with the Ministry of Finance. This was a clear indication that the Kim government would not follow the policy rationale of state-led development and that there would be no need for the Economic Planning Board, which was previously responsible for the five-year economic development plan and coordinating policies of different ministries, under the new government.

Overall, the Kim government intended to reduce state intervention in the market and to let economic actors make their own decisions (Chung 2003). Im points out that such a rationale of governance was influenced by the idea of new public management started by the Thatcher government in the UK (Im 2008). Around the early 1990s, Thatcherite new public management was spread all over the world by international organizations such the OECD and the World Bank, and the Kim government embraced the idea of new public management for its rationale of governance.

In practice, however, the Kim government followed the old rationale of the developmental state in its economic policy. For instance, the government launched the One-Hundred-Days Plan for economic recovery at the beginning of taking office. The Plan specified policy objectives such as the promotion of new strategic sectors and price management. It was a typical policy intervention of the developmental state, and contradicted what the Kim government intended to do at the level of policy rationale. The Kim government tried to reduce government intervention at the level of rationale of governance, but still resorted to the policy intervention of the developmental state at the level of implementation.

Due to such inconsistency, the government seemed to lose control of public affairs. There were high profile public accidents which should have been prevented by public agencies responsible for safety and security. One of the main bridges crossing the river at the center of Seoul and the building of an up-market department store collapsed due to shoddy construction and unauthorized renovation. The public safety agencies were blamed for negligence of their duties, and the business ethics of private sectors pursuing only profits were critically exposed. The public began to question government policy overall, which aimed to leave market actors to do whatever they might want.

The most dramatic catastrophe which hit Korean society hard was the East Asian economic crisis. The Kim government liberalized the financial sector and opened the financial market for international investors and financial institutions. Financial sector reform was implemented under the rationale of financial liberalization. It also aimed to dismantle government control of the banking sector, which was one of the hallmarks of the developmental state policy regime. With financial liberalization, international financial institutions began to operate in the Korean domestic market and Korean retail financial institutions got access to cheaper international monetary supply. It was later discovered that short-term capital with cheap interest rates borrowed from the international market was loaned to investors with higher interest rates in the longer term. It would have been money-making magic only if short-term capital was constantly supplied to replace previous borrowings. It was, however, a high risk operation with serious threat to the economy. The Ministry of Finance and Economy and the Bank of Korea failed to monitor the increasing vulnerability of the economy due to the financial liberalization.

In 1997, the East Asian financial crisis that started with the collapse of the Thai Baht manifested as panic momentum for international financial institutions to withdraw financial leverage from the Korean market. Because of the structural weakness of the retail banking sector, the Korean government could not cope with the sudden flight of international financial capital combined with the fall of Korean currency. Table 3.1 shows that the size of international debt in terms of GDP ratio and the amount of interest payment in terms of export ratio were not so large as in other East Asian countries hit by the crisis. In other words, the economic crisis in

Table 3.1 International debt burden (Unit: %)

	Korea	Indonesia	Thailand	Mexico
Debt/GDP ratio	25[1]	57	35	70
Interest payment/export	5.8[2]	30.9	10.2	12

Note Korean data points 1: 1997, 2: 1996. Other countries: 1995
Source World Bank (1997) cited in Chang (1998)

Korea amid the East Asian crisis was more to do with policy failure rather than a simple debt crisis. At the level of governance, while the Kim government tried to dismantle the policy regime of the developmental state and to opt for neo-liberal economic management, there was a clear void in terms of new institutional arrangements for neo-liberal governance.

Overall, the Kim Young-sam government tried to dismantle the policy regime of the developmental state and to establish a market-oriented liberal system. The economic growth was not so much the overriding goal as in the period of the developmental state. A political drive against corruption also significantly eroded the vested interest of the old guards of the developmental state such as military, bureaucracy and politicians. Despite such efforts, there was a clear internal inconsistency between the rhetoric and actual policy implementation. The practices of governance from the developmental state continued at times. The government dismantled those policy instruments of the past, but necessary systems were not in place, especially in the financial sector. Financial mismanagement and inexperience was spectacularly manifested during the East Asian economic crisis in 1997. It is, however, worth noting that the new regulations on real-name financial transactions and property registration provided crucial institutional infrastructure for political transparency and market efficiency, which were essential for the future development of governance.

3.4 State-Led Economic Reform and Social Protection

Long-time opposition leader and campaigner for democracy, Kim Dae-jung, won a historic victory in the presidential election of 7 December 1997, with 40.3% of the popular vote. It was for the first time a transition of power from the governing party to the opposition party. The election outcome was strongly influenced by the failure of the previous government and the subsequent East Asian economic crisis. While in the opposition party, Kim Dae-jung advocated political ideas of economic equality and political liberty and was expected to depart from the previous rationale of governance. He did not, however, have the freedom to pursue his own political programs as he came to the office of President in the wake of the economic crisis and had to accept policy recommendations from the International Monetary Fund (IMF) in order to secure the emergency loan necessary to cope with the financial crisis. The IMF and the Korean government agreed on the four main reform programs: reforms of the financial sector, corporate governance structure, labor market and public sector (IMF 1997). These were the reforms to change the Korean economic structure to be in line with the liberal market economy (Hall and Soskice 2001).

Even though the immediate cause of the economic crisis in 1997 was the financial liberalization that the government had tried to introduce, the IMF maintained the stance that Korea should continue the liberalization reforms. At the time of the crisis, the IMF as well as other policy commentators such as Greenspan, the

Federal Reserve Chairman, saw that political interventions resulted in misallocation of investment, and maintained that the policy regime should be reformed. In other words, they believed that the reform should be carried out to leave behind the developmental state as the rationale of governance.

In the financial sector following the IMF recommendation, the government-owned banks were to be privatized while some of the large banks were sold to international investors. The Financial Supervisory Commission was created to maintain market stability, keeping a certain degree of distance from the Ministry of Finance and Economy. The most difficult challenge was the labor market reform. Given the rising labor costs above the productivity increase with the strong labor movement in the 1990s, the previous government failed to carry out labor market reform before the economic crisis. The labor reform was intended to make the labor market more flexible, allowing firms to lay off their workers easier and to employ workers with non-regular contracts, meaning limited periods of employment or dispatch by primary employers. The reason the labor market reform was very difficult to implement was not only because the trade unions were strong and militant, but also because social protection for the unemployed was very weak.

Coming from the opposition party, Kim Dae-jung was able to convene a tripartite committee including the trade unions, business organizations and the government in order to forge a social consensus for the labor market reform. The reform required a significant concession from trade unions, and trade unions came to the negotiation table because of Kim's strong ties with them for many years. Through the social compact made by the tripartite committee, the new labor regulations were allowed to be implemented while the government would introduce a series of social protection measures including unemployment benefits. The Employment Insurance Program, introduced in 1995, had only covered a small section of employed persons and was extended to swiftly to cover more people. The government also implemented a series of public works projects from 1998, which provided short term jobs for 432,000 people in 1998 and 1699,000 in 1999 (MOGAHA 1999).

Kim Dae-jung government went further in its effort to strengthen the social protection system. A new program for poor households was introduced in 2000 and implemented in 2001. It was the Minimum Living Standard Guarantee which would provide minimum income to poor households as a social right and would be based on the concept of relative poverty. Fragmented public health insurance funds were integrated into National Health Insurance, while the National Pension Program was maintained as a public pension program despite the IMF recommendation for privatization.

In terms of public sector reform, the Kim government first reduced the number of public sector workers through voluntary early retirements and smaller recruit-ment. The second wave of public sector reform aimed to increase the accountability of public agencies and citizen satisfaction with their services. It followed the model of the Next Step Agencies implemented in the UK according to new public man-agement. It is also worth noting that the Ministry of Planning and Budget was re-established after being merged with the Ministry of Finance and Economy by the previous government.

The question from this observation is whether the Kim Dae-jung government really departed from the developmental state as the rationale of governance. In terms of state-society relations, the role of the government was still strong in implementing reforms. Although the Kim Dae-jung government implemented the reform programs recommended by the IMF, it was the government that led the reform process in order to cope with the economic crisis. The role of the government was also crucial in the efforts to upgrade the Korean economy with high technology and high value-added industries such as IT and shipbuilding. The difference is that the government began to use many indirect and sophisticated policy instruments such as supporting industries with venture capital and removing regulations. The Korean government controlled commercial banks effectively by using the new regulatory regime (Lee 2002). Labor market reform was based on social consensus rather than government unilateral push. Overall, the developmental state regime was substantially weakened as the new public management reforms were introduced in the government bureaucracy. In terms of policy goals, economic recovery and growth were juxtaposed with social protection and equity.

3.5 Participatory Democracy and Innovations in the Public Sector

Roh Moo-hyun was elected President in 2003, yet another victory for the center-left Democratic Party. His victory was described as a victory against the conservative ruling coalition and the vested interest of the Korean society (Ahn and Cheong 2007). Roh emphasized participatory democracy as the new rationale for his government and promised equitable development across the country. President Roh also maintained that the state should have an important role to play for economic development and participatory democracy.

The Roh government's main policy program was the relocation of the nation's administrative capital from Seoul to a newly planned city called Sejong. As a presidential candidate, he argued that there had been too much concentration in the metropolitan area of Seoul in terms of politics, public administration, business and culture. It was an inevitable outcome of Korea's rapid industrialization and social transformation, but Roh saw it as the social result of economic inequality and monopoly of political influence (Seong 2014). The move of the nation's administrative capital away from Seoul was a policy response to the monopoly of power and economic wealth.

Even though President Roh saw that the state should play an active part in distribution efforts in terms of income and spatial allocation of wealth, he did not resort to the hierarchical decision making of the bureaucratic structure. Instead his government established a number of Presidential Commissions, where different social stakeholders came together to forge social consensus on difficult policy issues. Among those Presidential Commissions, the most prominent were the Presidential Commission for the Relocation of New Administrative Capital and the

Presidential Commission for the Equitable Development of the Homeland. These Commissions coordinated government ministries as well as social stakeholders with different policy ideas.

Compared to the previous two governments, the Roh government did not reduce the size of the government or the number of civil servants. Rather, it emphasized the efficient working of the government and introduced various innovations for new public management. First the Roh government introduced the internal market system in which government agencies worked with other agencies more like market actors. Secondly, performance evaluation systems were introduced across the government ministries and incentives were given to high performers. Outside experts were allowed to join the civil service in 'Open Recruitment Positions'. Thirdly, the Roh government integrated an e-government system across the government such as e-procurement, e-immigration and e-document systems.

There were, however, criticisms about the initiatives of new public management. One senior civil servant pointed out that too many new measures and systems of innovation were introduced within a short span of time, and the government agencies and people working inside were confused by these new measures and systems (Park 2008). In the end, those new initiatives failed to produce the desired outcomes, at least in the short-term. The real blow to the Roh government's public sector reform came from politics. The National Assembly passed an impeachment bill against President Roh in 2004. The President was accused of unlawful political intervention in preparation for the general election scheduled in 2004. It was the first time in Korea that an impeachment of the President was attempted. Presidential power was suspended in March 2004 while the proceedings went on. After more than a month of proceedings, the Constitutional Court ruled that the impeachment of the President should be rejected, and Roh reassumed his office as President. Although the President was acquitted, the impeachment proceedings brought about a serious degree of confusion in the government and consequently many of the public sector reform programs went astray.

In terms of policy outcome, the Roh government failed to materialize what it tried to achieve. Despite policies for more equitable distribution, there was a rise in income inequality and the number of middle income jobs diminished during the tenure of the Roh government. The number of people with middle income jobs decreased while the number of people with low wage jobs increased (Cheon and Kim 2005). Such a trend was due to the labor market tendency to give favor to highly skilled workers compared to workers with a medium level of skills. Those workers were laid off through continual employment adjustments and fell into the lower income groups. These social economic trends contradicted the policy orientation of the government, and the middle and low income classes withdrew their political support for President Roh.

Instead of mobilizing all the efforts for economic growth, the Roh government placed more emphasis on social justice. It pursued equitable distribution of income and wealth across income groups and different regions. The Roh government's policy orientation was a clear departure from the developmental state. In terms of political power, the Roh government was an antithesis to the power elite of bureaucrats and big businesses which used to be the backbone of the developmental state. As a rationale of governance, the Roh government emphasized participation and deliberation, using participatory institutions including Presidential Commissions and tried to introduce innovative instruments to increase efficiency in bureaucracy. What do all these efforts add up to? It is true that the Roh government departed from the governance of the developmental state, but his government failed to leave an enduring legacy for a new rationale of governance since President Roh's minority government could not steer away from political turmoil, which prevented government policies from producing substantial results.

3.6   Back to the Developmental State?

Lee Myung-bak took the office of President in 2008. The conservatives, the Hannara Party, won a landslide victory against the Democratic Party's candidate. The Roh government failed to sustain political support due to worsening income inequality and polarization of the labor market. The majority of the electorate expected that incoming President Lee could restore economic growth with his experience in the private sector. He was one of the star executives at Hyundai Construction, which grew rapidly during the heyday of economic growth in the 1970s and 1980s. At times in the presidential campaign, Lee tried to project himself as the new President Park Chung-hee. Although the Presidential Transition Committee maintained that the new government would seek economic growth in tandem with social development (Presidental Transition Committee 2008), the policy priority was economic growth. The Lee government presented a low-carbon green growth strategy. It indicated that the government would encourage private business to develop green energy and to innovate new technology and skills in order to prevent global climate change. It would then be an economic engine for growth.

As the private sector failed to jump on the bandwagon of the green growth strategy, the Lee government requested government-owned public enterprises such as the Korea National Oil Corporation to acquire overseas oil wells to boost energy-related industries. The government also launched a massive infrastructure development project of the four main rivers across the country. The government spent a huge amount of public expenditure to develop the shore areas of four main rivers and to install many dams and reservoirs to control annual flooding. It was a typical Keynesian government spending program to stimulate the economy. The Lee government created a new super Ministry of Strategy and Finance to spearhead different ministries for the purpose. It merged the Ministry of Finance and Economy and the Office of Budget and Planning under the previous government.

In order to restore economic growth, the Lee government resorted to the policy rationale of the developmental state regime (Im 2014). The Lee government's strategy of the developmental state faltered due to the global economic crisis that started in New York and London in 2008. In order to tackle immediate economic challenges in the wake of the global economic crisis, the Lee government could not maintain a coherent rationale of governance. In 2010, the Lee government tried to reverse the policy of relocating the administrative capital, which was decided by the previous government. It was a bold attempt to restore policy initiatives, but the National Assembly rejected the government bill. It was an especially serious political blow to President Lee since Park Geun-hye, who was the leader of the governing party, led the National Assembly's rejection. In other words, the government was defeated by the governing party. After such a humiliating defeat, the Lee government lost their grip in terms of steering the nation's policy agenda.

In December 2012, Park Geun-hye won the presidential election. She came back to the presidential residence, the Blue House, which she had left after her father President Park Chung-hee was assassinated by his close adviser 33 years ago. There was a great expectation that she might rejuvenate the rationale of the developmental state in a democratic setting. As discussed in Chap. 2 Part II, her campaign was based on a manifesto that placed strong emphasis on social welfare. Her welfare initiative was understood as a completion of her father's modernization project. After three years in office, however, her government failed to make significant progress in terms of public reform, partly because the National Assembly blocked her government policy proposals and partly because she refused to make a political compromise.

3.7   Conclusion

This chapter has examined the reforms which the Korean government has carried out for the past three decades since democratization. It tried to answer the question of whether the Korean governments went beyond the policy regime of the developmental state and came up with a new rationale of governance.

The Kim Young-sam government introduced public sector reforms which aimed to reduce the size of the government and purged the old political guards in the army and the bureaucracy under the 'civilian' government. His government introduced institutional frameworks for banking transactions and real property registration, which were significant breakthroughs that provided institutional infrastructure for transparent market exchange against political corruption. Despite such efforts, the Kim government resorted to the old practice of the developmental state in economic policy when it was strained by the economic downturn, which created policy incoherency. Due to such incoherency and inexperience, the Kim government failed to deal with policy challenges arising from a new global environment, which turned out to be the most dramatic economic catastrophe in the form of the East Asian economic crisis.

The Kim Dae-jung government carried out structural reform in order to steer away from the economic crisis. In so doing, the government forged a social consensus through the tripartite committee. It was a clear contrast with the previous rationale of the developmental state in which top policy makers and government ministries predominated decision making. In order to implement the reform following the compromise made in the tripartite committee, the Kim Dae-jung government strengthened the welfare system. The existing social policies were strengthened and new programs were introduced to give better protection to citizens during the period of structural adjustment. Nevertheless, the Kim government did not depart completely from the old practice of governance. It also resorted to the old style of the developmental state when it promoted industries of high-technology such as internet and communications.

Following the efforts of the two previous governments, the public sector reforms under the Roh government were intended to depart from the rationale of the developmental state. Efforts were more thorough in terms of rationale of governance. Economic growth was not regarded as the overriding goal of public policy. Instead, the government pursued more equitable distribution in terms of income and regional development. In order to rebalance uneven development across the country, the Roh government initiated a move for the relocation of the administrative capital to Sejong city. In terms of state-society relations, new approaches such as participation of different stakeholders in deliberative decision making bodies were explored experimentally.

Despite these different government efforts, this chapter has shown that the developmental state still remains as a rationale of governance. The Roh government was often involved in political controversies including the impeachment trial of the President, which led to a failure to construct a solid rationale of governance. The Korean governments frequently resorted back to the old style of governance when the governments needed to respond to pressing policy challenges, especially economic difficulties. It is mainly because they failed to develop clear and coherent alternatives to the developmental state as the rationale of governance, and because it was the way the government could deal with the problems with confidence. Even though new public management was adopted at times, there was a lack of coherence and consistency in the adopted rationale of governance. At the same time, however, the developmental state as the rationale of governance has lost ground slowly but steadily over the last three decades amidst continuous and various public sector reforms.

When the conservative Lee government came back to power after two left-leaning governments, it was not a forgone conclusion whether the old rationale of governance would be restored or a new rationale of governance would be created. The Korean governments left the developmental state behind, but they failed to establish a coherent and consistent alternative for the following government to take. It is a challenging imperative for the upcoming Korean government in particular to find an appropriate rationale of governance for the future. Nevertheless, the groundwork for the challenge has been done. There are important building blocks which have been shaped by the Korean governments in their efforts toward public sector reforms over the last three decades.

The regulations on real-name banking transactions and property registration were a milestone for institutional infrastructure for transparency in market transactions. Political corruption and murky business dealings have been reduced in terms of size and number by these regulations, although it cannot be said that they have disappeared. The productive welfare initiative brought about extension and reinforcement of the welfare state in Korea. The concept of social rights is now firmly established together with political and economic rights. The idea of partic- ipatory and deliberative democracy was experimented with as a new mode of interest mediation. Economic growth still remains as one of the foremost policy objectives, even if it is not the most important goal. These building blocks were chosen because they are regarded as essential ingredients for the improvement of Korean society. The task for the future Korean government is to reconstruct a coherent rationale of governance using those building blocks, as they may conflict with each other without a clear overall framework.

It is also necessary to develop and elaborate an appropriate role for the government in economic and social policy. At the level of political rhetoric, each government except the Roh government maintained that the size of the government should be reduced and the area for government intervention should be minimized. At the level of practice, the government still plays a leading role in society-state relations. All in all, Korea has left behind the developmental state and it is necessary to develop a new rationale of governance.

References

Ahn B, Cheong M (2007) Democracy, equality and public administration. Korea Rev Publ Adm 41(3):1–40 (in Korean)

Amsden A (1989) Asia's next giant: South Korea and late industrialization. Oxford University Press, Oxford

Chang H (1998) Korea: the misunderstood crisis. World Dev 26(8):1555–1561

Cheon B, Kim B (2005) The labour market polarization and policy challenges: with focus on employment polarization. Labour Rev 7:36–51 (in Korean)

Choi B (2014) Managing conomic policy and coordination: a saga of the economic planning board. In: Kwon H, Koo MG (eds) The Korean Government and public policies in a development nexus, vol 1. Springer, New York

Chung C (2003) New understaning of public administration. Daeyoung Publishing, Seoul (in Korean)

Haggard S (1994) Macroeconomic policy and adjustment in Korea, 1970–1990. Harvard University Press, Cambridge, MA

Hall A (1993) Policy paradigms, social learning, and the state: the case of economic policymaking in Britain. Comp Polit 25(3):275–296

Hall P, Soskice D (2001) an introduction to varieties of capitalism. In: Hall P, Soskice D (eds) Varieties of capitalism: institutional foundation of comparative advantage. Oxford University Press, Oxford

Im T (2008) Philosophy of public administration. In Korea Institute of Public Administration (Ed) Sixty Years of Public Administration in Korea. Beopmoonsa, Seoul (in Korean)

Im E (2014) Critical analysis of the discourse of advancement under the Lee Government. Rev Gov Stud 20(2):355–396 (in Korean)

IMF (1997) Republic of Korea: IMF Stand-by Arrangement. From http://imf.org/external/np/oth/korea.htm

Johnson C (1982) MITI and the Japanese miracle: the growth of industrial policy, 1925–1975. Stanford University Press, Stanford

Kim B, Vogel E (eds) (2011) The Park Chung Hee era: The transformation of South Korea. Harvard University Press, Cambridge

Kwon H (1999) The welfare state in Korea: the politics of legitimation. Macmillan, London

Kwon H, Koo MG (2014) The Korean Government and public policies in a development nexus, vol 1. Springer, New York

Lane J (1987) Implementation, accountability and trust. Eur J Polit Res 15(5):527–546

Lee Y (2002) Debate on the emergence of the regulatory state in financial sector reform in Korea. Korea Sociol 36(4):59–88

Mkandawire T (2001) Thinking about the developmental States in Africa. Camb J Econ 25 (3):289–313

MOGAHA (1999) Report on Government's public works project. From http://www.mogaha.go.kr/works/index.html

Park CH (1963) The country, revolution and I. Hollym, Seoul

Park S (2008) Government innovation: outcome, reflection and challenges. Paper presented at the annual conference of the Korean Association of Public Administration, Seoul (in Korean)

Presidental Transition Committee (2008) Success and sharing: the whitepaper of the 17th presidential transition committee. Presidential Transition Committee, Seoul

Seong K (2014) New administrative capital and equitable development of the nation. In Korea Institute of Public Administration (ed) Rho Government: governance and main public policies of the Korean Governments. Daeyoung Publishing, Seoul (in Korean)

White G (1998) Constructing a democratic developmental state. In: Robinson M, White G (eds) The democratic developmental state: politics and institutional design. Oxford University Press, Oxford

Woo J (1991) Race to the swift: state and finance in Korean industrialization. Columbia University Press, New York

Woo-Cumings M (ed) (1999) The developmental state. Cornell University Press, Ithaca

Chapter 4
The State-Civil Society Relationship in Korea

Yeonho Lee and Chi Hoon Sung

4.1 Introduction

Since the occurrence of the financial crisis in 1997 and the emergence of the Kim Dae-jung Government, civic groups have started to show a conspicuous increase in their activities. For the Kim Dae-jung Government to pursue political and social reforms, it required not only the political support of progressive civic groups, but also non-profit organizations (NPOs)[1] that could provide social welfare services along with the government to manage the mass unemployment that resulted from the financial crisis. In line with Korea's democratization, civic groups displayed quantitative expansion as well as qualitative growth. Furthermore, the political influence that non-governmental organizations could exert was also enhanced. Since the civilian government came into power, civic groups have often professed to be the vanguard of political, social and economic reforms, and the government used a partnership strategy to take full advantage of the situation.

Do these signs of growth in the civic groups in Korea provide evidence of a civil society more autonomous from state power? To be more precise, is the relationship between the government and civic groups in Korea escaping from the statist model with little social welfare spending and a small non-profit sector, and moving

---

[1]Non-profit civic organizations (NPOs) are civil society organizations that serve public interests by producing or providing quasi-public goods such as education, medical treatment, culture and social services for development and welfare for society. This research uses the term NPO to refer to non-profit foundations that do not seek profit in legal terms (educational foundations, social welfare foundations, and scholarship foundations, etc.) as well as civil society organizations.

Y. Lee (✉) · C.H. Sung
Yonsei University, Seoul, South Korea
e-mail: yhlee@yonsei.ac.kr

C.H. Sung
e-mail: summits83@naver.com

© Springer International Publishing AG 2017   47
J. Choi et al. (eds.), *The Korean Government and Public Policies*
in a Development Nexus, The Political Economy of the Asia Pacific,
DOI 10.1007/978-3-319-52473-3_4

towards a liberal model with little social welfare spending by the government but yet with an expanded non-profit sector that manages welfare and advocacy services which the government cannot?

Regarding such questions, this research shows that there has still been an imbalance between state and society in Korea since 1998. What matters the most is that the relationship between the government non-governmental organizations is not a horizontal and equal one. Although this relationship is framed as very independent and objective, it consists of a two-fold structure in which non-governmental organizations are seized under government influence in return for support from the government including financial subsidies.

The theories which presume the emergence of a civil society have their basis in the hypothesis of modernization theory. This theory insists that as a state becomes economically abundant, it will lead to the growth of a bourgeois citizen class that is affluent and well-educated. As a result, the theory assumes that this would lead to the development of liberalism and democracy, and ultimately the reduction of state power and the establishment of a free market and civil society from an evolutionary perspective (Hall and Gieben 1992; Fukuyama 1992). But despite political democratization, sustained economic development and the resulting rise of a prosperous civil class, Korean government and society still displays a hierarchical and subordinate relationship with the state at its apex. For instance, there is a strong tendency toward a statist model, with the government not providing much social welfare expenditure and small non-profit groups. Furthermore, there is a high possibility that the civic groups could remain as a 'collaborative vendor' model where they simply carry out government programs with government funding, rather than a 'collaborative partner' model where the civic groups could exercise significant freedom in the management and development of their programs.

This research aims to examine aspects of government-civic group relations in Korea by analyzing the relationship between the government and non-profit civic organizations. It is necessary to include the market mechanisms within civil society such as businesses and labor unions (Kim 1997) when defining what civil society is. However, the research will limit the boundary to exclude the economic sector and focus only on the public sector or the non-profit sector in order to prevent the research from crossing into overly broad realms. The relationship will also be analyzed by focusing on the statistics of government-provided funding to non-governmental organizations. Unfortunately, the statistical data are difficult to interpret accurately. This is because government funding provided to non-governmental organizations is not managed under a unified system, but is administered by the central government and local governments, respectively. Even within the central government, various departments have provided the funds, and the departments themselves have gone through changes among different governments and time periods. This has resulted in a lack of systematic data management. This research analyzes non-profit private organization support programs conducted by the Ministry of Public Administration and Security, among the various non-profit private organization support programs initiated by the Kim Dae-jung Government. This is because the data provided by this program offers the most consistent statistical data compared to the others. The research covers the period from 2000, when it became possible for the government to provide financial support to civil society groups under the Act on Assistance for Non-Profit and Non-Governmental Organizations, to 2015, under the Park Geun-hye Government.[2]

4.2 Theoretical Discussions

The advent of autonomous civil society and the consequent gradual downscale of the state is the basic assumption of modernization theory. Modernization theory postulates the advent of a citizen class due to the expansion of economic wealth, the demand for political rights to protect individual property, and the accompanying development of liberalism and democracy. Modernization theory-based thinking, which proposes that the most evolved form of state-society relationship is one that develops with the latter at the center, forms the foundation of civil society theory, which is essential to this research.

Salamon and Anheier suggested the three-sector theory model, which categorizes the relationship between the state and the non-profit sector into statist, liberal, social democratic and corporatist by setting the level of the state's social welfare expenditures as one axis and the size of the non-profit sector as the other (Table 4.1).

First, the corporatist model is a situation in which the state has a high level of social welfare expenditure and the size of the non-profit sector is also big. To alleviate the private sector's pressure on social welfare, the state intervenes and works with churches or landed aristocracy to stimulate them to engage in philanthropic programs. In this situation, the social welfare expenditure of the state and the size of the non-profit sector increase in direct proportion. A statist model is one in which the state's social welfare spending is low and the size of the non-profit sector is also low. In this model, the state exercises influence superior to society, but it comparatively refrains from speaking for working class interests in patriarchal means. The government's social welfare activities and the non-profit sector's programs both show contraction. The social democratic type is one in which the government's social welfare expenditure is high, but the size of the non-profit sector is small. Because the state actively performs social welfare activities, the non-profit sector faces limits in the scope of its programs. Lastly, the liberal type is one in which the social welfare spending of the state is low, but the size of the non-profit sector is large. It can be interpreted that in this type, the private sector's intentions

---

[2]The Ministry of Public Administration and Security has disclosed the data since 2008, so the previous data from 2000 were collected by using the data from the parliamentary inspections. In the case of 2006 and 2007 under the Roh Moo-hyun Government, data on the number of programs and the total amount of funds were included, but the data on each subcategory could not be acquired and thus were excluded. Still, it would be fair to say that there will not be much difficulty in identifying the overall outline of the research and government dispositions.

Table 4.1 Analysis based on the three-sector model

Scale of the government's social welfare expenditures	Size of the non-profit sector	
	Low	High
Low	Statist	Liberal
High	Social democratic	Corporatist

Source Salamon and Anheir (1998: 228)

to remain vigilant against excessive expansion of the state sector lead to the expansion of the non-profit sector (Lee 1998: 44).

The three-sector theory model does not refer to which type of relationship is the most preferable between the government and non-profit civic groups. However, scholars in this field generally agree that it is desirable for non-profit organizations to possess a significant level of autonomy in the management and development of their programs, and not to depend excessively on government financial aid. These scholars suggest that although there should be room for state support in early developmental stages, it is ultimately desirable for the groups not to financially depend on the government, but rather to pursue a collaborative partnership in order to secure an independent realm from the state (Joo 2001: 66–68). Of course, according to political and social conditions, there are countries where a strong tradition of dualistic model remains, such as the United Kingdom. In the United Kingdom, the education sector developed through a collaborative model with government financial assistance. On the other hand, the government-dominant model was shown with the state directly intervening (Joo 2001: 48). Nevertheless, a remarkable trend is taking place worldwide towards a 'collaborative partner relationship' in relation to the expansion of civic society. The collaborative partner relationship is being established not only in liberal countries such as the United Kingdom and the United States where the private sector has traditionally had power, but also in conservative corporatist countries such as Germany.

The collaborative partner relationship postulates that the government and non-governmental organizations keep a relatively close relationship with each other. In the sense that non-profit organizations administer formerly state-managed programs through state funding, the two maintain a collaborative relationship. Therefore, an essential precondition for a collaborative partner relationship is a strong and autonomous private sector in the substructure of society that stay abreast of the government sector.[3] If a collaborative relationship is pursued without meeting this precondition, it is highly probable that the non-profit organization will lean closer to becoming an interest group. Even if the state and the non-profit sector carry out their

---

[3]Collaborative-vendor, which is in contrast with collaborative-partner, means a 'relationship in which the NPOs fail to have discretionary power or negotiating power and end up as agents of the government which carry out government programs with government resources. Whether the relationship is collaborative-vendor or collaborative-partner relationship depends on the level of discretionary and negotiating power that the NPO with government fund can exercise' (Lee 1998: 46–47; Girdon et al. 1992).

respective programs without a collaborative partner relationship, non-governmental organizations should be guaranteed autonomy from the influence of the government sector if they are to keep a complementary or supplementary relationship with the government.

Meanwhile, the aspired models of democracy for the respective governments should also be taken into account along with the types of government-civil society relations. Even when the governments were all aiming to achieve democracy, they prescribed different levels of civil society participation in the state sector according to their different specific models. In analyzing the Korean case, it is necessary to approach the problem using the participatory democracy model and the legal institutional democracy model. The two models display differences according to the levels of democracy in political and social dimensions. The deepening of democracy, which takes place by expanding democratic logic in not only the political sphere but also the social and economic spheres, causes institutional changes in democracy. As more weight is placed on the value of equity rather than freedom, the scope and intensity of democracy deepens from "legal and formal democracy" to "participatory democracy." Legal and formal democracy postulates the "elimination of excessive intervention by the state against competition", the "downsizing of the political power of interest groups", and the "establishment of a strong state which could enforce law and order" (Hayek 1976; Held 1987). In contrast, participatory democracy supposes that "all classes of the society would equally participate in policy decisions without discrimination." It creates a situation in which "citizens directly participate in the regulation of the society's major institutions", and in which "equal rights to develop oneself" and "distribution of material resources" are guaranteed (Pateman 1970). While the former limits the application of democratic logic to the political realm to a certain extent, the latter shows a tendency to extend and apply the logic, not only to the political but also to the social and economic realms.

Legal and formal democracy aims to liberate the market and society from unnecessary intervention from the state, but to strengthen state ability to supervise and regulate the market. Its goal is to make the relationship between the state and the market objective, in which they do not collude with each other. From a political and economic perspective, the model is largely in accordance with new right wing or neo-liberal paradigms which suggests a small yet strong government. The model aims to establish a government or a state which possesses the capacity to set and enforce policies effectively.

On the other hand, participatory democracy respects the freedom of market and society, but shows differences from the earlier model in that it allows political intervention of the government against the market to a certain extent and social intervention against government and market through civil participation in order to improve equality among different social classes and industries. In particular, it is important to note that the model aims to accumulate social capital by fostering civic organizations as the third sector in addition to the state and market (Putnam 1993). The state induces civil society and economic society (in other words, the market) to develop policies through which they can cooperate, rather than engage in conflict.

While the legal and formal democracy model perceives the state-market and state-society relationship as mutually conflicting, the participatory democracy model supports a position of coexistence and symbiosis by pointing out that a strong society should be a prerequisite for the establishment of a strong state, and hence a strong (namely effective) market (Evans 1997: 62–87).

4.3 Government-NPO Relationships Under Progressive Governments

Before democratization in 1987, civil society organizations in Korea were mostly under government control. Groups with great social impact received financial support from the government and accepted legal and political regulations from the government as well. They mostly acted as an agent of the government, performing activities needed by the government on its behalf. Such a tendency to keep civic groups under government control persisted to a certain degree until the Kim Young-sam Government, which was referred to as the first civilian government after Park Chung-hee's Yushin Regime. In short, the government tried to utilize civic groups as the *avant-garde* of government-intended democratic social reforms.

The Kim Dae-jung Government also tried to make use of civil society organizations as the government's amicable supporter to obtain legitimacy as a democratic government, win political support from the people, and collect public opinion. There were clear negative opinions against the Kim Dae-jung Government's support of civic groups. Above all, such critics pointed out that a citizen movement supported by the government cannot but collude with the ruling party and/or government officials. In fact, when the government financially supports a non-profit organization which is voluntarily established, there is a possibility that a symbiotic interdependent relationship could develop through the former's internalization of the latter (Lipsky and Smith 1989: 625–648). Nevertheless, the Kim Dae-jung Government adhered to the position that it is natural for the government to financially assist civil society organizations, as civic groups are inadequately supported in Korea. It also pointed out that in cases of advanced nations such as the United States, not only the government but also private foundations actively support non-profit organizations; therefore, financial support by the government could diversify the financial base of civic groups, thus allowing them to perform activities in a more stable manner (Ferris and Graddy 1989: 127–128).

Since the Kim Dae-jung Government, government support for civil society organizations has rapidly increased. It increased from 84.4 billion KRW(US $70.8 million) in 1990 to 286 billion KRW(US$240 million) in 1998—4 times in nominal price and 2 times in real price. This increase was bigger than the government budget increase of 230% (in terms of nominal price) during the same period (Kim 2000a, b: 87). Such a drastic rate of increase coincided with the enactment of the Act on Assistance for Non-Profit and Non-Governmental Organizations in late 2000 by the Kim Dae-jung Government. The legislation supported NGOs by institutionalizing financial and administrative support to private organizations. For a more consistent and systematic analysis, the funds provided by the Ministry of Public Administration and Security under the Kim Dae-jung and the Roh Moo-hyun governments are organized and presented in Table 4.2. Overall, the Kim Dae-jung Government tended to more actively provide support compared to the Roh Moo-hyun Government. While the number of support programs gradually increased under the Kim Dae-jung Government, it gradually decreased under the Roh Moo-hyun Government. Also, the amount of funds provided under the Kim Dae-jung Government were relatively consistent with an average of 7.5 billion KRW(US\$6.3 million), while it started decreasing from the second year of the Roh Moo-hyun Government and ultimately remained at 4.9–5 billion KRW(US\$4.1–US\$4.2 million).

The detailed categories of support programs provided by the Ministry of Public Administration and Security under the Kim Dae-jung Government are laid out in Table 4.3.[4] From 2000 to 2002, the programs most emphasized by the Kim Dae-jung Government were those related to expansion of citizen participation, social integration, and growth of human rights and civic interests. This was in line with the Kim Dae-jung Government's pursuit of participatory democracy through expanding citizen participation in policy decisions, enhancement of harmony by increasing social equality, and pursuit of civil rights to achieve non-authoritarian politics.

As identified, the motive behind the Kim Dae-jung Government's support of non-profit organizations was their poor financial status with no suitable sponsor other than the government. Major civic groups, with the exception of the People's Solidarity for Participatory Democracy (PSPD) which started its activities without government support from the beginning, could barely operate with only membership fees. According to a survey of non-profit organizations in 2000, private organizations in Korea covered 39% of their budgets with membership fees on average, and received 19% of their budgets from local governments and public institutions. They also covered 19% of their budgets with donations from individuals, firms, foundations and other organizations, while the amount of funds secured through profits from activities and other fees accounted for only 12% of their budgets (Institute of East and West Studies, Hankook Research 2000).[5]

---

[4]Because there are differences in program categories according to various governments and periods, this research reorganized program categories with the same characteristics into a single category to identify the changes that took place. The 10 reorganized categories are as follows: (1) Social integration, (2) Expansion of citizen participation, (3) Cultural civil rights movement, (4) Volunteer work, (5) Growth of human rights/interests, (6) Establishing social transparency, (7) Resource saving/environmental preservation, (8) Safety supervision/disaster relief, (9) Assisting North Korean citizens/overseas Koreans, (10) International exchanges.

[5]Although a direct comparison could not be drawn, this shows stark contrast with non-profit social service organizations in the United States, which earned 47.0–57.11% of their budgets through self-sustained activities such as program costs and fees while receiving less than 10% of their budgets from government funding (Rho 2001).

Table 4.2 Changes in the number of programs and amount of funds, 2000–2007

Government	Kim Dae-Jung government			Roh Moo-Hyun government				
Year	'00	'01	'02	'03	'04	'05	'06	'07
No. of programs	195	216	237	237	154	158	148	155
Amount of fund (billion KRW)	7.5	7.5	7.5	7.5	5	4.9	4.9	4.9
Average amount provided (million KRW)	38.46	34.72	31.65	31.65	32.47	31.01	33.11	31.62

Source Parliamentary Inspection Material, Korean National Assembly (2000–2007)

Table 4.3 Ranking of weights given to each specific category, 2000–2002 (Unit: %)

Rank	Content	Weight	Rank	Content	Weight
1	Expansion of citizen participation	17.26	6	Cultural civil rights movement	8.56
2	Social integration	16.35	7	International exchanges	8.50
3	Growth of human rights/interests	12.91	8	Assisting North Korean citizens/overseas Koreans	5.47
4	Resource saving/environmental preservation	11.73	9	Establishing social transparency	5.27
5	Volunteer work	10.21	10	Safety supervision/disaster relief	3.73

Source Parliamentary Inspection Material, Korean National Assembly (2000–2002)

Furthermore, the Kim Dae-jung Government tried to avail itself of civic groups as a tool and *avant-garde* power for reform in a political dimension as well. The Kim Dae-jung Government, which put forward 'democracy and market economy' as its political and economic motto, pushed ahead a set of reforms against the chaebol in the economic sector by using the 1997 financial crisis as momentum. According to the perspective of progressive power, the chaebol were behind the centralization of economic power with poor financial structure, and were immoral economic groups that monopolized immense economic wealth (Kim and Kim 1999).

In political terms, the government attempted to pursue the so-called Sunshine Policy, a policy of engagement with North Korea, and reforms to reorganize the political establishment. The progressive power needed socio-political support to undermine the conservative power, and civic groups were considered a political resource that could offer assistance to the government. In 2001, for example, the government carried out a tax audit against the conservative media, which was then deemed to be untouchable. In the judicial process, scandal was unearthed related to tax evasion, inheritance and false circulations. This led to wide criticisms against the government both domestically and internationally. They suggested that the government was engaging in political retaliation for the conservative media's criticisms about the government's progressive North Korean policies. However, the government was able to enforce procedure with the support of civic groups which advocated government-led media reform policy.

The pattern shown in the support programs led by the Ministry of Public Administration and Security under the Roh Moo-Hyun Government did not differ much from those under the Kim Dae-jung Government. There were only slight differences in the ranking of the programs supported by the government, with social integration, expansion of citizen participation, and growth of human rights and interests occupying the biggest share. The two similar pursuits of the two governments can be attributed to their similar ideologies (Table 4.4).

The reason social integration programs were emphasized most under the Roh Moo-hyun Government was directly related to the preceding government's goal of improving equality and welfare. In particular, the Roh Moo-hyun Government greatly highlighted improvement of welfare as its aim. Criticism was mounted against the preceding Kim Dae-jung Government which argued that the gap between the rich and the poor increased while overcoming the financial crisis under the IMF's free market prescription. The Roh Moo-hyun Government explicitly tried to surmount this criticism.

Therefore, the social welfare expenditure under the Roh Moo-hyun Government showed a drastic increase compared to the pre-financial crisis period (refer to Chap. 2). In the same context, as identified in Fig. 4.1, the share of social welfare expenditure in the government budget also tended to increase throughout the Roh Moo-hyun Government. The reason behind the increase of the social welfare expenditure ratio under the Roh Moo-hyun Government was demand for an increased social safety net due to the deepening of economic inequality during the process of overcoming the financial crisis. This policy orientation of the Roh

Table 4.4 Ranking of weights given to each specific category, 2003–2005 (Unit: %)

Rank	Content	Ratio
1	Social integration	18.90
2	Expansion of citizen participation	15.54
3	Growth of human rights/interests	14.38
4	Cultural civil rights movement	13.35
5	Resource saving/environmental preservation	12.97
6	Safety supervision/disaster relief	9.19
7	Volunteer work	7.09
8	International exchanges	6.18
9	Establishing social transparency	2.40
	Total	100

Source Parliamentary Inspection Material, Korean National Assembly (2003–2005)

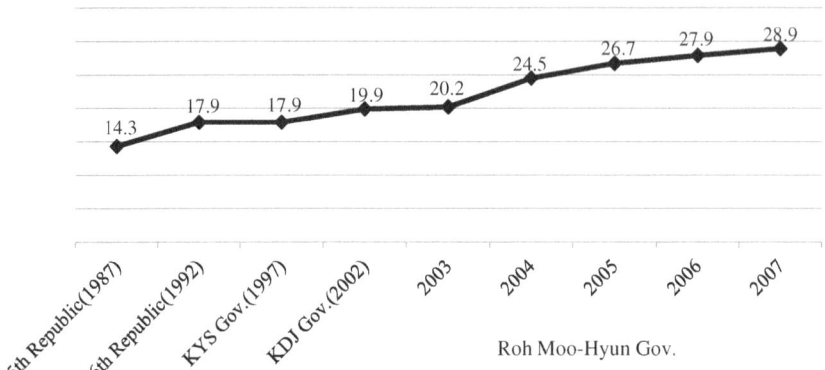

Fig. 4.1 Share of social welfare expenditure in the budget (Unit: %). *Source* National Statistics Office

Moo-hyun Government led to an emphasis on social integration programs among the various support programs of the Ministry of Public Administration and Security.

The Roh Moo-hyun Government strongly promoted policies that facilitated the participation of non-profit civic organizations, just as the preceding government had done. It tried to equally reflect the interests of different classes in policies by including as many civil society powers as possible in policy decision processes. Unlike its predecessor, the Roh Moo-hyun Government actively encouraged the participation of labor movements. The Kim Dae-jung Government had promoted the participation of progressive civil society groups, but did not actively extend the targets to include labor forces as well. Although the Federation of Korea Trade Unions and the Korean Confederation of Trade Unions were legalized after the February 8th Social Contract in 1998, they were neglected by the government and did not become a class power.

The Roh Moo-hyun Government, however, valued not only civic groups but also the labor class as partners and expanded the political support base by including them in policy decision process. When he became the president-elect, Roh Moo-hyun involved a large number of experts from civic groups and the labor class in his presidential transition committee. Furthermore, the Roh Moo-hyun Government selected and pursued "labor-management relations that promote social integration" as one of the 12 agenda points for national administration. This was an effort to raise the voices of the labor force by giving them leverage, as the labor class had until then been relatively disadvantaged. In the structuring of the government cabinet, the ratio of personnel from the labor class, especially those from the Korean Confederation of Trade Unions, was much higher compared to other governments (Lim 2004).

In addition, the Roh Moo-hyun Government revitalized the political participation of civic groups to reform the conservative-centered power structure and solidify its weak political base. Such effort by the Roh Government was clearly displayed in the advancement of major personnel from civic groups into government posts. 36.1% of former and incumbent executives of PSPD, a major civic

Table 4.5 Public posts of PSPD executives entered under various governments

	Kim Young-sam	Kim Dae-jung	Roh Moo-hyun	Others	Total
Presidential panel	6	48	63	4	121
Prime minister's panel	0	16	16	3	35
Departments in government	5	27	51	5	88
Legislation	1	5	3	3	12
Jurisdiction	1	1	2	1	5
Independent organization	6	13	21	2	42
Local government	3	3	2	2	10
Total	22	113	158	20	313

Source Lew and Wang (2006)

group in Korea, entered *Cheongwadae*, high-ranking government posts, and various government-affiliated committees. As observed in Table 4.5 above, 50 former and incumbent executives of PSPD held posts in 63 of the 121 presidential organizations (52.1%). There was a sharp increase in number, even when compared to the Kim Dae-jung Government (48 organizations). 5 personnel from PSPD were included in the Presidential Secretariat (Lew and Wang 2006). Also, according to an analysis of 84 former and incumbent Policy Advisers to Ministers in the Roh Moo-hyun Government, there were 10 members of civic groups, accounting for 11.9% of the total number (Lee 2013: 227).

To sum up, although the state-civic group relationship seemed to change into a collaborative partner relationship after democratization, this was not necessarily the operational relationship in reality. In fact, the collaborative vendor or statist model showed a much higher level of relevance in the case of Korea. In short, there was a phenomenon of civil society organizations' subordination to the government. Of course, it is not possible to explain this phenomenon by generalizing all civic groups. For example, PSPD did not receive government support at all but was observed to exercise a comparatively high level of autonomy. Nevertheless, many conditions were lacking for a collaborative partner relationship to be established between the government and civic groups overall. Most of all, the non-governmental organizations were deprived of ways to acquire financial independence. Therefore, they could not help but depend on government support for the management and maintenance of the organization.

4.4 Government-NPO Relationships Under Conservative Governments

In February 2008, the ten years of progressive regimes under Kim Dae-jung and Roh Moo-hyun came to an end, giving way to a conservative regime. Unlike the progressive regime which legislated the Act on Assistance for Non-profit and

Non-Governmental Organizations, there were concerns that the conservative regime would not maintain support for non-profit civic organizations Moreover, it was predicted that the autonomy of non-profit organizations would further deteriorate in a context where the state-society relationship did not fully develop into a liberal model.

However, in contrast with these predictions, the conservative government maintained support for civic groups and the amount of funds and number of support programs actually increased after the middle phase of Lee Myung-bak Government. How can we understand such a phenomenon? To begin with the conclusion, an increase can be identified in the amount of funding and the number of groups. However, when examining the details of the conservative government's financial support for non-profit civic organizations, it becomes clear that civic group autonomy did not expand. In fact, their autonomy and objectivity actually declined.

First of all, the scale of the Ministry of Public Administration and Security's public programs for non-profit civic organizations in the Lee Myung-bak Government's first year in 2008 maintained nearly the same category and amount of funds, because it was already outlined under the previous regime. The average amount of funds provided to each organization decreased in 2009 when the new government autonomously conducted the program. However, the number of support programs, amount of funds, and average amount of funds provided to each organization showed a tendency to gradually increase overall. In comparison, the total amount of funds and average amount of funds provided to each organization tended to decrease in general under the Park Geun-hye Government as it approached its middle phase (refer to Table 4.6).

The Lee Myung-bak Government's stand on civil society organizations was originally set by the massive candlelight rallies in 2008. Large scale candlelight rallies persisted nationwide in regards to renegotiations concerning the import of American beef. Numerous progressive civil society organizations participated in the rallies. The government labeled the so-called mad cow disease candlelight rallies as unlawful and violent, and announced that it would restrict government support for the civic groups that participated in the rallies. In February 2009, the National

Table 4.6 Changes in the number of programs and amount of funds, 2008–2015

Government	Lee Myung-bak government					Park Geun-hye government		
Year	2008	2009	2010	2011	2012	2013	2014	2015
No. of programs	133	162	158	220	293	289	293	223
Amount of funds (billion KRW)	4.9	4.9	4.9	9.8	14.78	14.48	13.27	9.0
Average per organization (million KRW)	36.84	30.25	31.01	44.61	50.44	50.10	45.29	40.36

Source Ministry of the Interior (2008–2015)

Police Agency sent an official document to each government department with the title: "Information on the current status of groups related to unlawful violent demonstrations in 2008." Most government branches including the Ministry of Public Administration and Security excluded the non-profit civic organizations in the official document as fund recipients (Jwa 2011: 226–227).

In this context, the basis for government support of civic organizations changed greatly. In 2009, programs of focus in the previous regime such as social integration, expansion of citizen participation and growth of human rights and interests were eliminated. Instead, support was given to programs in line with the government's main policies including the 100 national administration agenda, job creation, the Four-River Restoration Project, and low-carbon green growth. The Lee-Myung-bak Government's decision to increase support for non-profit civic organizations according to its policy directions was against the basic direction of the Act on Assistance for Non-profit and Non-Governmental Organizations, which stipulated that the state should "respect the inherent domain of non-profit civic organizations" and actively make efforts so that non-profit civic organizations could "exercise their creativity and expertise to participate in activities related with public interests."

As non-profit private organizations and the opposition party raised criticisms against the government's position, the programs returned to their previous categories in 2010. For instance, the "social integration and welfare enhancement" category received the most amount of support, as it did in 2008. However, after 2011, the Lee Myung-bak Government again changed its stance to provide more support for organizations which were likely to support the government. Although the amount of funds provided increased to 9.8 billion KRW(US$8.2 million), twice the previous amount, the recipients were expanded with conservative civil society groups at the focus. Regarding this, there were criticisms that the government was supporting conservative groups bearing the general election and presidential election in mind. In fact, "national security and public safety" programs started rapidly increasing as shares of total funds from 2011, eventually making up 26.71%, the highest ratio of all subcategories, in 2012 (refer to Table 4.7).

As a whole, the programs that received the most support under the Lee Myung-bak Government were "social integration and welfare enhancement,"

Table 4.7 Total weights placed on each subcategory, 2008–2012 (Unit: %)

Rank	Content	Weight
1	Social Integration and welfare enhancement	24.22
2	Cultivation of advanced citizenship	16.46
3	National security and public safety	15.53
4	International exchange and cooperation	14.08
5	Environmental preservation and resource saving	13.77
6	National administrative goals	11.90
	Total	100

Source Ministry of the Interior (2008–2012)

"cultivation of advanced citizenship," and "national security and public safety" (refer to Table 4.7). "Social integration and welfare enhancement" accounted for the highest share of the total support provided. Because "social integration," "growth of human rights/interests," and "assisting North Korean citizens/overseas Koreans" were independent categories under the progressive governments that have been combined into this single category, it should be noted that the ratio of integration and welfare programs actually did not increase, but maintained its previous level. Social integration and welfare programs were already emphasized under the previous progressive government. These programs received a lot of attention from all governments, both conservative and progressive, as industries went through restructuring programs after the Asian financial crisis in 1997 and the US-triggered global financial crisis in 2008.

The conservative government, which promoted flexible market policies, also set the procurement of a social safety net as its agenda. But when looking at other support program categories, the Lee Myung-bak Government showed a tendency to support non-governmental organizations that sided with its ideological values, as the Kim Dae-jung Government had done. The Lee Government required the conservative citizen class to ideologically support it. This can particularly be seen in the rapid growth of "national security and public safety" programs in the late phase of the government, as the program included many conservative civic groups. The Lee Myung-bak Government aimed to expand the influence of conservative civic groups which had been relatively disadvantaged under the progressive regime, by providing them with financial support.

The Park Geun-hye Government, which shared a similar conservative ideological disposition with the Lee Myung-bak Government, did not display much difference in its support to the respective categories. The top three categories with the highest amount of funds provided were the same as those of the Lee Myung-bak Government. The difference was that the "national security and public safety" category received the most support with a higher share occupied in the total amount of support. As can be identified in Table 4.8, the weight placed on the "national security and public safety" category continuously showed high figures, recording 25.8% in 2013, 24.88% in 2014 and 28.54% in 2015. A stark contrast can be found

Table 4.8 Total weights placed on each subcategory, 2013–2015 (Unit: %)

Rank	Content	Weight
1	National security and public safety	26.21
2	Social integration and welfare enhancement	22.73
3	International exchange and cooperation	20.50
4	Cultivation of advanced citizenship	13.42
5	Environmental preservation and resource saving	11.30
6	National administrative goals	3.11
7	Public economy and cultural development	2.73
	Total	100

Source Ministry of the Interior (2013–2015)

when comparing the figures with the Kim Dae-jung and the Roh Moo-hyun governments. "Safety supervision/disaster relief", which was analogous with "national security and public safety" under the progressive government classification, ranked at the bottom under the Kim Dae-jung Government with 3.73%, and recorded only 9.19% under the Roh Moo-hyun Government. Such difference can be interpreted as a phenomenon that occurred when the Park Geun-hye Government increased support for security and military-related civic groups, which strongly endorsed the administration.

Another characteristic visible in the relationship between the Lee Myung-bak and the Park Geun-hye governments and civil society organizations was that support for major conservative groups increased. These included the National Council of the *Saemaul* Movement, the Association for the Society for a Better Tomorrow, and the Korea Freedom Federation. The pretexts for subsidies provided to these groups were "building a bright and healthy state and society" and "cultivating mature liberal democratic values". These three groups had subsidized their operating expenditures according to regulation under a special act[6] before legislation related to the Act on Assistance for Non-profit and Non-Governmental Organizations under the Kim Dae-jung Government in January 2000. The subsidies received integrated management after legislation enacted by the Kim Government. However, the Lee Myung-bak Government reclassified the National Council of the *Saemaul* Movement in 2009 and two other organizations in 2010 as those excluded from subsidies under non-profit civic organizations, public interest activities, and designated them as "organizations that directly receive national subsidy programs." This was an effort to increase support for the groups with strong tendencies to support the government.

The total amount of funds received by the three organizations in the 10 years before their direct subsidization was 7428 million KRW(US$6.2 million), which accounted for 11% of the 67 billion KRW(US$56.3 million) assigned as the Ministry of Public Administration and Security's support program expenditures. There were already criticisms that the amount of funds provided to these three organizations was excessive compared to other civic groups. However, despite the criticisms, the Lee Myung-bak Government arranged an institutional basis to enable more support for these organizations by designating them as directly subsidized organizations. As can be seen in Table 4.9, the amount of funds received by the groups after they were directly subsidized was higher than the total amount they had received in the 10 years before their status change. This is a tendency that persisted until very recently. The three organizations were funded a total amount of 2167 million KRW(US$1.8 million) in 2015. Considering that the total amount of funds provided to 233 civic organization programs under the Ministry of Public

---

[6]The special act for the three organizations means legislation related to the National Council of the *Saemaul* Movement, The Association for the Society for a Better Tomorrow and Korea Freedom Federation.

Table 4.9 Changes in the amount of funds provided to the three interest groups

	2000–2009 (million KRW)	After direct subsidization (million KRW)	
National council of the Saemaul Undong movement	3882	2009	3000
		2010	1990
		2011	2390
The association for the society for a better tomorrow	1395	2010	1000
		2011	1000
Korea freedom federation	2151	2010	1000
		2011	1000
Total	7428		11,380

Note The numbers indicate the total amount of funds for the National Council of the *Saemaul* Movement from 2000 to 2008, and the two other organizations from 2000 to 2009
Source Jwa (2011)

Administration and Security was roughly 9 billion KRW(US$7.6 million) and the organization that received the highest amount of funds during the period (Youth Forum of North Korea Democratization) was supported with 240 million KRW(US $0.2 million), it is not difficult to realize that the scale of the funding provided to the three groups was huge.

Overall, the total amount of funds allocated by the Ministry of Public Administration and Security to non-profit civic organizations during the 8 years of conservative governments increased by 50% compared to the same number of years under progressive governments (excluding 2006 and 2007). The amount of funds allocated to each program also increased by nearly 10 million KRW(US$8400). But one cannot conclude that this increase in the amount of government-provided funding did not contribute to the expansion of civic group autonomy. Rather, these organizations' dependence on the government and government intervention into civil society groups increased together with the increased amount of funding.

To sum up, as can be seen in Fig. 4.2, the Kim Dae-jung and Roh Moo-hyun governments mainly supported social integration, expansion of citizen participation,

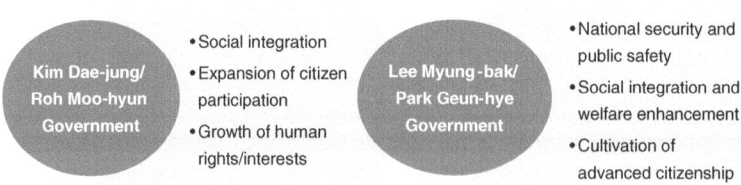

Fig. 4.2 Changes in support program categories between progressive/conservative governments

and growth of human rights/interests programs, while the Lee Myung-bak and Park Geun-hye governments mainly supported national security and public safety, social integration and welfare enhancement, and cultivation of advanced citizenship programs. As a result, the state-civic group relationship could not advance into a collaborative partner relationship under the Lee Myung-bak and Park Geun-hye governments, and actually displayed more similarities to the statist model. Support for non-profit civic groups increased 1.5 times in quantitative terms, but the state-society relationship still showed imbalance. It would be more appropriate to interpret the increase in the amount of funds as an increase in costs to nurture non-governmental organizations supportive of the government.

4.5 The State-Society Relationship from the Perspective of the Government and Non-profit Civic Organization Relationship

As we have seen above, after the enactment of the Act on Assistance for Non-profit and Non-Governmental Organizations by the Kim Dae-jung Government, governments expressed they would legally, institutionally and financially support non-profit civic groups in establishing a collaborative partner relationship with them. But it is inevitable to be somewhat skeptical on the question of whether such an idealistic relationship was established. The relationship established between the two sides was merely artificially presented to resemble a cooperative one, but did not actually reflect reality. Although the governments indicated the relationship would promote an autonomous collaborative partnership on the surface, it has been shown that the reality is more of a collaborative vendor relationship or even a government-dominant model.

The dual aspects of the state-civic group relationship in Korea result from the fact that the rise of civil society groups did not come from the advent of an autonomous civil society, but was necessitated by the political needs of the authority in power. The fundamental reasons why non-profit civic organizations rapidly grew under the Kim Dae-jung and Roh Moo-hyun governments, which claimed participatory democracy, can be summarized into two points. First, the two governments needed non-profit civic organizations to carry out reforms by politically pressuring establishments such as the chaebols and the conservative political power. They gained support from the middle and the labor classes, and used the civic organizations as the *avant-garde* of progressive political reform and the political supporter of the government. Secondly, the people viewed civic campaign organizations as alternative political representatives of existing political parties, which failed to collect and express public interests adequately.

On the other hand, the conservative Lee Myung-bak and Park Geun-hye governments, which aimed to achieve legal institutional democracy, chose to block the revitalization and political participation of the progressive civil society organizations as much as possible. As a result, the amount of funds provided to non-profit civic organizations by the Ministry of Public Administration and Security increased in quantitative terms, but these funds were mostly channeled to conservative civil society groups which supported the two governments at the rear. A relatively lower amount was provided to progressive civil society groups with a critical stance toward the government and a disposition toward active political participation.

In political and economic terms, Korea could not prepare the necessary conditions for a collaborative partner model to be established. In Korea where the state-led developmental model had been upheld since the 1960s, the existence of an authoritarian state created a relatively daunted civil society and a market that lacks autonomy. A state-led economic system was disbanded after the Asian financial crisis in late 1997 and a transition towards a market-oriented or private-oriented system started. However, a strong state revived after the end of the crisis and civil society again contracted. The characteristics of the developmental state lingered, and the role of the welfare state was strengthened to secure a social safety net to support the unemployed due to persistent economic recession and the resulting industrial restructuring (Lee 2000). For these reasons, the collaborative partner relationship visible in liberal countries was advocated on the surface, but in reality civil society actually performed tasks on behalf of the state or was even subordinate to the state.

Then what is the fundamental and historical reason the government and non-governmental organizations cannot achieve a horizontal relationship in Korea? Countries like Korea belonging to the influence of Confucianism aim to reach an alternative modernization distinct from western modernization. The characteristics of modernity emphasized by the Confucian countries are moral loyalty rather than economic profit, governance by the wise rather than public political participation, and establishment of social order by courtesy rather than by law (Lee 1997). The medium which binds the relationship between the modern state and society in Korea is not economic-egoistic profit, but immaterial factors like moral loyalty and courtesy. Owing to the lingering of these historical institutional factors, it is difficult to adequately explain the state-society relationship in Korea using the western model, which categorizes the relationship in terms of expressing and organizing material profits between the two.

Of course, it cannot be said that these Confucian modernization factors still completely dominate the modern Korean state and society. It is true that these factors were weakened and replaced through the introduction of western modernity. Still, the influence of these informal institutions significantly remains and is affecting the formation of the state-society relationship in Korea. Although not discussed in this research, an appropriate example would be the state-market relationship. In the early stages of economic development grounded on a developmental state model, the government nurtured strategic industries and firms through various forms of support including financial support. As the impact of the business sector and the social sector expanded due to economic development and political democratization, the state-market relationship also faced pressure to gradually transform into an equal relationship. Nevertheless, the state-market relationship still could not overcome its hierarchical structure. It is maintaining a collaborative partner relationship on the surface, but the market is still substantially the subject of control and regulation by the state. With the advancement of economic liberalization, government regulations to supervise the market increased in qualitative and quantitative terms, while those on industrial support more or less decreased.

The market is a part of civil society, and if we assume that non-profit civic organizations are as well, then their autonomy with regard to the state cannot be other than very limited in Korea. Modernization theory, which supposes that a free citizen class will emerge as economic abundance and political democratization develop, is showing quite a high level of preciseness in Korea's case. But limitations also exist. More than anything, a bourgeois class armed with a liberal ideology has not developed as much as expected. There is still a strong tendency for citizens to depend on the state when problems occur. Virtues of civil society such as freedom, autonomy and self-governance are not respected enough. A lot of weight is still placed on the government or the state, compared to the individual or the citizen. State-centric thinking is still prevalent. In Japan, where civil society developed ahead of Korea, the relationship between the government and civic groups does not differ much from the Korean case. The financial self-reliance rate of Japanese civic groups is mostly around 20–30% and they receive support from local government or firms. Japanese civic groups have no choice but to establish cooperative relationships with the government and firms for their survival. Therefore, fierce competition among civic groups is taking place to win projects commissioned by the government or firms.

As long as Korean civic groups continue their financial dependence on the government, it is impossible for them to be independent of the government's political influence. Social power could relentlessly receive pressure to politicize and fail to remain as a pure non-governmental organization. Expecting social power to resist the state and preserve a high level of autonomy will remain difficult as long as a structure remains in which the hierarchical state can benefit from hierarchical authority. Also, it is predicted that more time would be required for non-governmental civic organizations to develop and maintain a collaborative partner relationship with full autonomy from the state. The autonomy of non-governmental organizations from the state will therefore always be somewhat limited as long as the hierarchical properties of the state-society relationship remain.

References

Evans P (1997) The eclipse of the state? Reflections on stateness in an era of globalization. World Polit 50(1):62–87

Ferris JM, Graddy E (1989) Fading distinctions among the nonprofit, government and for-profit sectors. In: Hodgkinson VA, Lyman RW (eds) The future of the non-profit sector. Jossey-Bass Publishers, San Francisco

Fukuyama F (1992) The end of history and the last man. Penguin, London

Girdon B, Kramer R, Salamon L (eds) (1992) Government and the third sector: emerging relationships in welfare states. Jossey-Bass Publisher, San Francisco

Hall S, Gieben B (eds) (1992) *Formations of Modernity*. Polity, Cambridge

Hayek FA (1976) The road to serfdom. Routledge and Kegan Paul, London

Held D (1987) Models of democracy. Polity, Cambridge

Institute of East and West Studies, Hankook Research (2000) Research report on the current situation of Korean private organizations (in Korean)

Joo SS (2001) Argument about civil society and NGO: main idea, model and theory. Hanyang University Press, Seoul (in Korean)

Jwa S (2011) Changes in non-profit non-governmental organizations support project during the Lee Myung-bak government. Citizen and World 19:223–236 (in Korean)

Kim I (1997) Nonprofit sector and NGOs: definition, classification and research methods. J East and West Stud 9(2):5–35 (in Korean)

Kim I (2000a) From cleavages to accommodation: the political economy of consociational democracy and neo-corporatism in the Netherlands and Austria. Korean J Int Stud 40(4):225–250 (in Korean)

Kim J (2000b) The growth of the non-government sector in Korea and its relations with the state. Paper presented in Northeast Asian Civil Society: current status and challenging roles of NGOs in Korea, Japan and China (2000, November 11), Seoul

Kim D, Kim K (1999) Reform theory of chaebol in Korea. Na-nam Press, Paju (in Korean)

Lee Y (1997) The state, society and big business in south Korea. Routledge, London

Lee H (1998) History and structural characteristics of NGO. J East and West Stud 10(2):42–75 (in Korean)

Lee Y (2000) The Kim Dae-jung governments economic reform and limitations in the rise of the Neo-Liberal state. In: Wilkinson R, Maltby J, Lee J (eds) Responses to change: some key issues for the future of Korea. University of Sheffield, Sheffield

Lee Y (2013) Unequal development and democracy. Pakyoung Press, Seoul (in Korean)

Lew S, Wang HS (2006) PSPD report. The Center for Free Enterprise (in Korean)

Lim Y (2004) Study on political participation of the labor union in Korea: focusing on 'participatory' government. Master's thesis, Yonsei University, Seoul (in Korean)

Lipsky M, Smith SR (1989) Non-profit organizations, government and the welfare state. Polit Sci Q 104(4):625–648

Pateman C (1970) Participation and democratic theory. Cambridge University Press, Cambridge

Putnam DR (1993) Making democracy work: civic traditions in modern Italy. Princeton University Press, Princeton

Rho YH (2001) Changes in revenue resources of nonprofit social service organizations. Korean Association of Nonprofit Organization Research, 2001 Autumn Conference Published Thesis (November 23) (in Korean)

Salamon L, Anheir H (1998) Social origins of civil society: explaining the nonprofit sector cross nationally. Int J Voluntary Nonprofit Organ 9(3):213–248

Part II
Public Policies Beyond the Developmental State Paradigm

Chapter 5
The National Innovation System (NIS) for the Catch-up and Post-catch-up Stages in South Korea

Keun Lee, Buru Im and Junhee Han

5.1 Introduction

Since the 1960s, South Korea has achieved outstanding economic growth. It has been very successful in catching up to the level of advanced countries and has become a good example of 'compressed growth', in which a country achieves rapid development in decades that took more than a century in developed countries. However, rapid economic growth was not simply a smooth progress as there were crises, like in the mid-1980s when Korea lost export competitiveness due to rising wage rates. Internally, a rise in wage rates in the domestic market led to an increase in production costs. Externally, Southeast Asian countries started to export similar products at cheaper prices. This led South Korea to fall into the so-called middle income trap. It occurs when a country is not innovative enough and thus fails to produce high-priced differentiated products, while at the same time there are countries which produce similar goods at lower production costs. This phenomenon is considered to be a very important topic in many institutions such as the World Bank (World Bank 2010).

One of the reasons why South Korea and Taiwan were able to overcome the middle income trap and reach the level of advanced countries is the high R&D investment that took place from the mid-1980s (Lee 2013). Since that period, the ratio of R&D investment to GDP has surpassed one percent, and among total R&D investment, private R&D investment has become higher than public R&D

This chapter is a further revised and translated version of the author's article published as Chap. 2 of Lee et al. (2014) written in Korean.

K. Lee (✉) · B. Im · J. Han
Department of Economics, Seoul National University, Shillim Dong, Seoul 08826, South Korea
e-mail: kenneth@snu.ac.kr

investment (Lee and Kim 2010). The experience of Korea and Taiwan suggests that the fundamental solution to overcome the middle income trap is innovation capability that enables countries to make qualified differentiated products through technological innovation (Lee 2013).

In this light, the source of innovation capability is a very important subject for countries, and many have consulted the concept of the national innovation system (NIS) developed by the Schumpeterian school of thought. Lundvall (1992) defines NIS as "elements and relationships which interact in the production, diffusion and use of new, and economically useful, knowledge." That is, NIS is a concept relating to the efficiency of the production, diffusion and use of knowledge. Scholars from the Schumpeterian school such as Lundvall and Nelson have advocated the NIS concept, arguing that differences in NIS among countries give birth to differences in innovation performance and thus countries' economic performance. In this sense, Schumpeterian economics differs from the mainstream economics which emphasizes the political institution; for instance, Acemoglu and Robinson (2012) suggested that political institutions determine the growth rate of countries, particularly inclusive institutions rather than extractive institutions. This argument cannot be generalized because political institutions are binding only in pre-modern societies or low-income countries but not necessarily in upper-middle- or high-income societies. By using the number of granted US patents and R&D expenditure as a proxy for innovation, Lee and Kim (2009) find that innovation capability is more important for economic growth in countries beyond the middle-income stage, whereas political institutions are binding for economic growth in lower-middle- or low-income countries.

Thus, while rapid economic catch-up of Korea can be better explained by its improved NIS since the mid-1980s, now in the 21st century when some catch-up has been achieved, its growth momentum is slowing down. So, it is time to review the past NIS adopted by South Korea for the catching up growth stage and suggest a new NIS more suitable for the 21st century or post-catch-up stages. In other words, this chapter aims to discuss the reform of NIS in South Korea so that it may sustain economic growth. The reform of the NIS can also be seen in the broad context of the shift of the growth model, such as from an imbalanced to a balanced one. The 'imbalanced catch-up' model which South Korea pursued in the 20th century was led by coalitions of big businesses in export-oriented manufacturing sectors and an activist government. In contrast, civil society and small and medium enterprises in mostly domestic market-oriented or service sectors have been left behind. As the economic growth of South Korea is now tending to slow down, more notably since the 2010s, it needs to reform the old imbalanced catch-up model and shift to a more balanced model, which can be called a 'co-catch-up' model.

The next section describes briefly the methodology for analyzing NIS, as we need to learn about some variables that can reveal various aspects of NIS. Then, Sects. 5.3 and 5.4 discuss NIS in the catch-up stage and NIS suitable for the post-catch-up stage, respectively. Finally, Sect. 5.5 concludes the chapter by suggesting policy options.

5.2 Methodology for Analyzing the NIS of Countries

Empirical analysis of innovation and knowledge is challenging because of the difficulty in measuring innovation and knowledge, and the lack of data. However, patent data have increasingly become available and used for this purpose because they, especially patent citation data, can be considered as a proxy for the paper trail of knowledge flows. Like academic articles citing each other, patent citations are about which patents cite which other patents, and are presumed to be informative links between patented inventions. In other words, knowledge flows among inventors leave a paper trail in the form of citations in patents (Jaffe et al. 1993). By conducting a survey of inventors, Jaffe et al. (2000) investigate the extent to which patent citations actually reflect knowledge flows and find that a significant proportion actually do. This finding makes it possible to use the probability of citation as a proxy for the probability of a useful knowledge flow.

A methodology has been developed for quantifying NIS by using patent citation data extracted from the US patent database, and here we will briefly introduce it and explain the usage.[1] In the Korean patent system, only recently has the database included information regarding which patent cited which other patents, but the US Patent and Trademark Office has been collecting citation data for a long time. Citation data of patents represents how existing knowledge is used for subsequent inventions, and thus contains valuable information for the flow of knowledge (acquisition and usage). For this reason, patent citation data is useful for innovation system studies trying to capture efficiency in the creation and usage of knowledge.

Jaffe and Trajtenberg (2002) provide extensive US patent data for researchers conveniently in the form of a CD. Their book also contains a description for the data and methodologies for econometric analysis using patent data. In comparing the NIS of countries, it would be problematic to use patent data from different patent offices because they use different standards. Thus it is important to use patent data collected by a particular country to which the largest number of other countries apply for patents. The US patent data is a perfect example of such a case, and thus we use patents filed in the US by Korea, Taiwan, Germany and other countries for international comparison. Now let us introduce the main variables describing NIS, which were also used in Lee (2013).

The first NIS variable is related to the source in the acquisition of knowledge and the degree of localization in the production of knowledge. That is, it regards how much knowledge being created relies on foreign or domestic knowledge bases. In other words, it measures how much knowledge is created domestically by citing the patents owned by inventors of the same nationality. It can be referred to as a measure of the localization of knowledge creation and is a proxy for how often the patent filed by a country cites other patents filed by its citizens. At firm level, it can be self-citation of patents belonging to a firm and is a variable that represents how independently firms produce knowledge. According to Lee (2013), Korea and

---

[1]For further details on the methodology, please refer to Lee (2013).

Taiwan showed a low degree of localization in knowledge creation in the early 1980s, which was similar to that of other middle income countries but much lower than that of advanced countries. However, the degree increased rapidly after the mid-1980s and reached the average level of advanced countries by the late 1990s, indicating a significant catch-up in this regard.

The second NIS variable regards the concentration of actors or patent holders in knowledge creation. It regards whether the producers of knowledge are led by a few big businesses or evenly distributed among a variety of inventors. Clearly, this variable shows a quite even distribution of knowledge producers for advanced countries while knowledge creation is concentrated with a few inventors in the case of typical developing countries.

The third variable for NIS is originality. Existing literature describes it as how wide the range of the source of knowledge is when a patent cites preceding patents. That is, we say that knowledge has a high degree of originality if it relies on knowledge from a variety of fields. Similar to the concentration variable, advanced countries show a relatively higher degree of originality than developing countries. Interestingly, countries from Latin America show higher degrees of originality compared to South Korea and Taiwan (Lee 2013).

The fourth variable for NIS is related to whether or not countries specialize in sectors with fast obsolescence of knowledge or slow obsolescence of knowledge. This notion is expressed as the cycle time of technologies. It represents the length of the life expectancy of the particular knowledge being used. A short cycle time of technology means that the life span of the knowledge lasts only a few years and after that the usage declines dramatically as it soon becomes outdated or less used. Cycle time of technology is calculated by measuring average time lags between the application (grant) years of the citing and cited patents. That is, it means how much on average a patent relies on old technologies for invention of new knowledge. Lee (2013) shows that major advanced countries are specialized in sectors with relatively longer cycle times of technology, while South Korea and Taiwan have shown a tendency to focus on sectors with relatively shorter cycle times of technology since the mid-1980s, as their patents tend to cite relatively recent patents.

The fifth variable for NIS is technological diversification. This regards whether countries or firms produce patents in a wide variety of fields or in a few limited areas. Lee (2013) shows that advanced countries have a higher degree of technological diversification than developing countries. In the case of South Korea and Taiwan, the degree of technological diversification has increased since the mid-1980s. Although it was still lower than that of German or Japan, the degree of technological diversification for South Korea and Taiwan has reached the average of high-income countries.

Using the above five variables, one can describe and analyze the innovation system at the country level as well as at the firm level (Lee 2013, Chap. 5) by measuring proper variables at each level. In addition, this method can be applied to analyze the sectoral innovation system by measuring sector-level variables. For example, Park and Lee (2006) find that catching-up countries, such as South Korea and Taiwan, have registered many patents in sectors associated with short cycle times of technology, while advanced countries have registered patents in sectors with relatively longer cycle times of technology. Park and Lee (2006) argue that this difference in technological specialization has contributed to successful catching-up for South Korea and Taiwan. Using the defined variables, this chapter distinguishes the differences between catching-up NIS and NIS suitable for an advanced country, and compares the NIS of South Korea with the NIS of other countries.

5.3 The NIS During the Catch-up Stages in Korea

Lee (2013) investigates the major characteristics of the catch-up stage NIS by comparing the NIS of South Korea and Taiwan with the NIS of both other developing and developed countries. He uses the above five variables to empirically test the determinants of per capita income growth. Additionally, he defines these variables at sector level and investigates which sector would be easier or more difficult for catching-up to take place. Finally, using firm data of South Korea and the US, he shows how Korean catching-up firms are different from the US firms in terms of objectives, behaviors and determinants of outcome. One of the most important results from this firm-level, sector-level and country-level empirical analyses is that successful catching-up countries and firms have specialized in sectors with short cycle times of technology.

The reasons that specializing in sectors with short cycle times is more advantageous for catching-up growth are explained in the following. First, specializing in fields with short cycle times of technology means that existing knowledge becomes obsolete fast. This would mean lower entry barriers for latecomers because they can afford to rely less on the existing knowledge dominated by advanced countries. Second, having short cycle times of technology, as in information technologies, means that new technology arrives more frequently, resulting in high growth potential. Additionally, specializing in sectors with short cycle times of technology would facilitate quickly raising the degree of knowledge localization (measured by self-citation at the country level). That is, it would be advantageous in achieving fast and successful localization of knowledge creation because reliance on old or existing knowledge controlled by advanced countries would be relatively low.

In country-level empirical studies, Lee (2013) demonstrates that there is a significant correlation between having more patent applications in fields related to shorter cycle times of technology and a higher per capita income growth rate, such as in Asian countries including Korea and Taiwan. In contrast, economic growth in high income countries as well as in other middle-income countries, is positively related to specialization in technologies with long cycle times, although they differed in that advanced economies specialized in high value-added sectors (e.g. pharmaceuticals), and other middle income countries, in low value-added sectors (e.g. apparels), within the long cycle technologies. At firm level, Lee (2013, Chap. 5) empirically verifies that Korean firms hold more patents in fields with shorter cycle times of technology compared to the US firms, and that having more patents in short cycle times of technology was significantly related to profit rates in Korean firms.

This finding suggests that specializing in sectors with short cycle times of technology is a way to avoid direct competition with advanced countries, and provide a niche market for latecomer countries with a certain profit rate. On the other hand, in the case of the US firms, the empirical study shows no significant relationship between cycle time of technology and firm performance. The self-citation ratio, which represents independent intra-firm mechanisms of knowledge creation, shows a positive and significant correlation with variables for firm performance such as firm productivity and value. This implies that the catching-up firms and mature firms have very different corporate innovation systems. These results indicate a different growth mechanism in place for catching-up and mature economies (Table 5.1).

Lee's study considers many variables representing innovation systems of various dimensions. These include the cycle time of technologies, originality, localization of knowledge creation, innovator concentration, and technological diversification. The study also identifies key variables responsible for growth and catch-up in a number of latecomer economies. Two variables, originality and concentration, did not pass the test. Economies that were successful in catching up and other developing countries did not differ in their accounts. In contrast, we find that the degree of knowledge localization and technological diversification in economies that have successfully caught up has rapidly increased over time. At the same time, such countries have specialized increasingly in short-cycle technologies. Thus, these three variables seem to hold the key to the question of the mechanism of economic catch-up.

As discussed above, they also appear to occur together and to complement each other. Statistically, there is a very high degree (as high as 0.7) of correlation between knowledge localization and technological diversification. In contrast, the variable of cycle time does not show such a high correlation with either of the two variables. Also, while advanced countries all tend to show high degrees of

Table 5.1 Determinants of economic growth in groups of countries

	Four Asian countries (Catching-up NIS)	High-income countries (Mature NIS)	Middle-income countries	World
Cycle time	(−)*	(+)*	(+)*	(+)*
Localization	+	(+)*	+	(+)*
Originality	+	+	+	+
Concentration	(−)*	(−)*	(−)*	(−)*
Four Asian Country dummy		(+)*	(+)*	(+)*
Other controlled Variables	Initial income, population growth rate, investment, middle and high school enrollment rate			

Source Regression summary table from Lee (2013, Chap. 3)
* in the cells indicate 10 percent significance level

knowledge localization and technological diversification, they all seem to have more patents in long-cycle technologies, which is exactly the opposite of the case with successful catching-up economies. Although the variable of knowledge localization shows rapid increases over time in catching-up economies, the variable is significant to performance only in advanced economies and their firms, whereas it was too low to be significant in middle income countries. The nature of technological diversification appears similar to that of knowledge localization. Based on this information, we take both diversification and localization as the end-state variables and the cycle time as an effective transition variable that guides us to end-state (Lee 2013: 213–214).

Before the mid-1980s, South Korea and Taiwan specialized in sectors with low-end, long cycle times of technology such as textiles or clothing. Since the mid-1980s, however, they have started to enter industries with short cycle times of technology such as electronics, semi-conductors, signal equipment and digital TVs. As a result, they accomplished technological diversification by entering a variety of industries, and at the same time, the degree of localization of knowledge creation continued to rise. To sum up, consecutive entry into sectors with short cycle times of technology resulted in technological diversification, and specializing in sectors with short cycle times of technology also made firms rely less on the technology of advanced countries, enabling them to achieve fast and successful localization of knowledge creation.

Lee (2013) also asks an intriguing question: did policy makers in these countries have short cycle times firmly in mind as they planned and implemented industrial policy? (Lee 2013: xvii). While the simple answer to this question is no, policy makers were in fact always asking themselves: "what next?" They looked keenly into which industries and businesses were likely to emerge in the immediate future and thought carefully about how to enter these emerging markets. Without specifically planning to do so, in effect the policy makers were always pursuing newly emerging industries which turned out to be short-cycle industries as these were often the ones that relied least on existing technologies. So far, we have been discussing catching-up NIS. Successful catching-up countries such as South Korea and Taiwan accomplished the desired level of catching up by specializing in sectors associated with short cycle times of technology.

In contrast, the degree of concentration and originality for those countries is not very different from other developing countries. Thus, Lee argued that the degree of concentration and originality is not the main element for catching-up growth. However, it is also established that the top-tier high-income countries all tend to have a more even distribution of inventors or less concentration, as well as high originality in their patent portfolios. This fact could mean that South Korea may also need to improve on these aspects or to switch to the NIS more typical for top-tier advanced countries. This issue is explored in more detail in the following section.

5.4   Transition to NIS for the Post-catch-up Stage

First, let us consider the trend of the average cycle time of technologies specialized by Korea, shown in Fig. 5.1. The Y axis in Fig. 5.1 depicts the average cycle time of technology represented by the US patents filed by Korean inventors. For instance, the number 10 on the vertical (Y) axis means that the average cycle time is 10 years, which in turn means that the patents filed by a country cite other patents that are ten years old on average. Thus, a smaller value (years) means that a country produces patents with a shorter cycle time of technology on average. This figure supports the turning point hypothesis that Korea, as a successful catching-up country, has gone through two turning points (Lee 2013). The first turning point occurred around the mid-1980s. Starting from this period, South Korea started to apply for patents in fields with shorter cycle times of technology, such as IT, resulting in a decrease of the average cycle time of technology. This is what happened during the catch-up stage.

Around 2000 or since the post-catch-up stage, however, one can observe the second turning point where the average cycle time of technology increases. This reflects a new trend that Korean firms are getting into technologies with longer cycle times (Fig. 5.1). The implication is that the catching-up stage is completed or a transition to the post-catching-up stage is occurring. Korean firms are thus getting

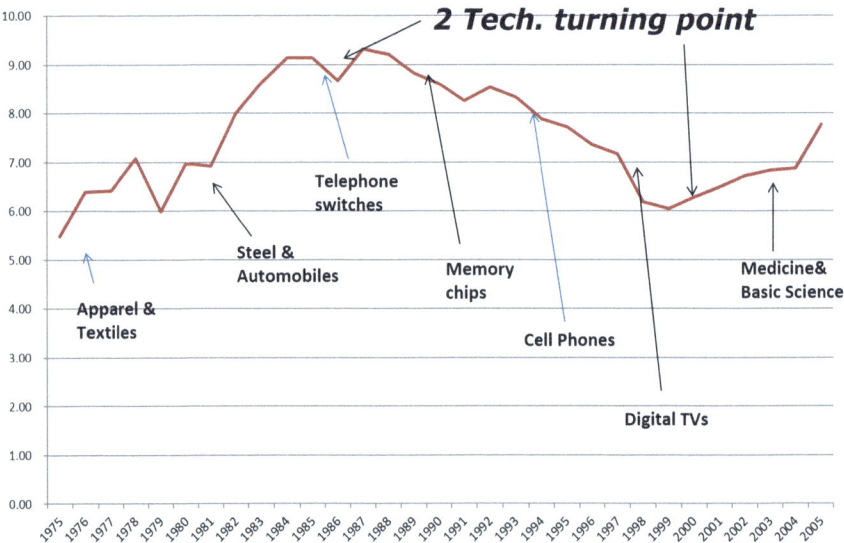

Fig. 5.1 Average cycle time of technology in Korean patents filed in the US and two technological turning points. *Note* The numbers in the vertical axis represent the average cycle time of the US patents registered by Korea. It is the average of differences in application years between the citing patents and cited patents. Higher value of this indicator means the patent relies on older technologies. *Source* Drawn using statistical data from Lee (2013)

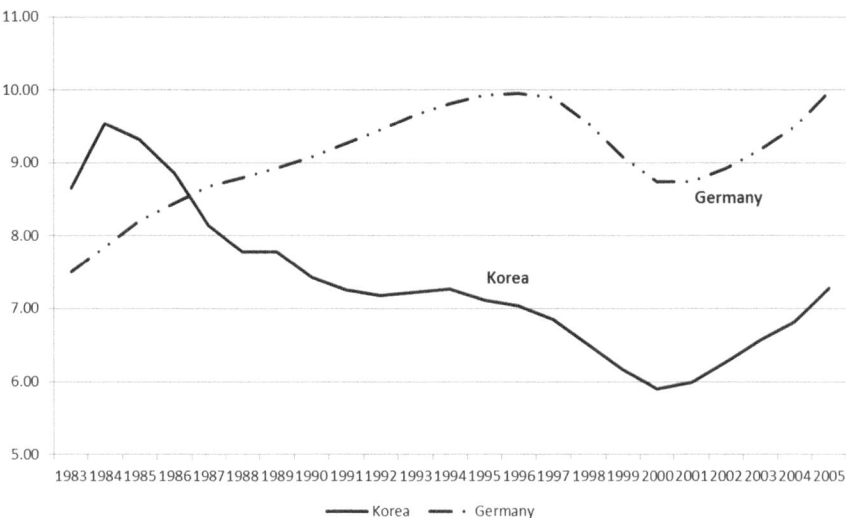

Fig. 5.2 Average cycle time of technology in selected countries. *Note* The numbers in the vertical axis represent the average cycle time of the US patents registered by each country, which is the average of differences in application years between the citing patents and cited patents. Higher value of this indicator means the patent relies on older technology. *Source* Statistical data from Lee (2013)

into technologies similar to top-tier advanced countries such as basic sciences, pharmaceuticals, and biotechnologies. While this is a good sign, international comparison indicates that Korea still has a long way to go. Figure 5.2, for example, shows that the average cycle time of technology for South Korea since the 2000s is much shorter than for Germany.

In terms of technological diversification, South Korea and Taiwan have a similar level of diversification, but are still not as diversified in comparison to that of Germany (Fig. 5.3). Figure 5.4 shows that the degree of originality of South Korea is higher than that of Taiwan, but is still lower than that of Germany. Figure 5.5 depicts the degree of concentration for South Korea, which is excessively high compared to other countries. This is because knowledge production and patent registration mainly come from a few big businesses in South Korea. As one can see, there is a big difference compared to advanced countries such as Germany. Interestingly, compared to Taiwan the degree of concentration is much higher in South Korea. Lee and Yoon (2010) show the reason behind this. Knowledge production in Taiwan is led by a variety of small and medium-sized firms.

Finally, Fig. 5.6 shows the degree of localization of knowledge creation. Germany has a high degree of localization of knowledge creation followed by Taiwan, and lastly South Korea. This suggests that South Korea needs to further increase the degree of localization of knowledge creation in order to become a top-tier advanced country. Lee and Yoon (2010) find the reason why South Korea has a lower degree of localization of knowledge creation than Taiwan: because the

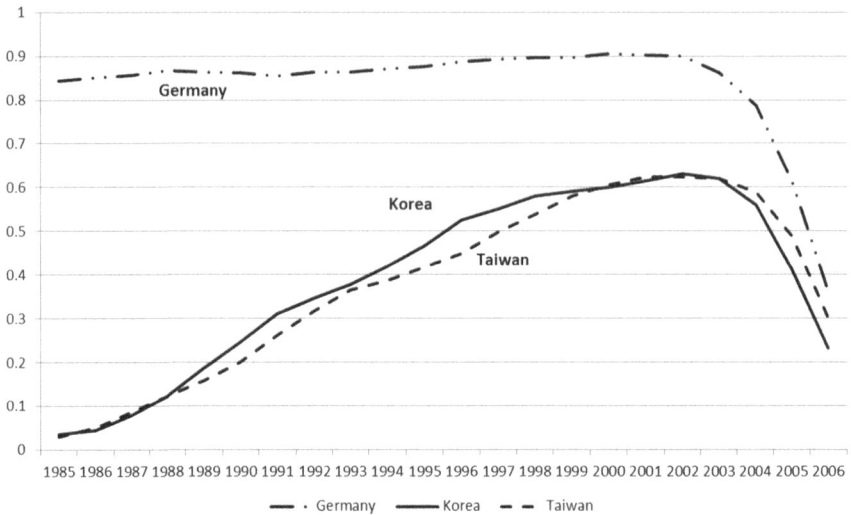

Fig. 5.3 Technological diversification in selected countries. *Note* Technological diversification is calculated by dividing the number of technology classes of patents applied for by a country in a year by the number of whole technology classes which is 417. Higher value of technological diversification means that the country in that year applied for patents in more various technology classes. *Source* Statistical data from Lee (2013)

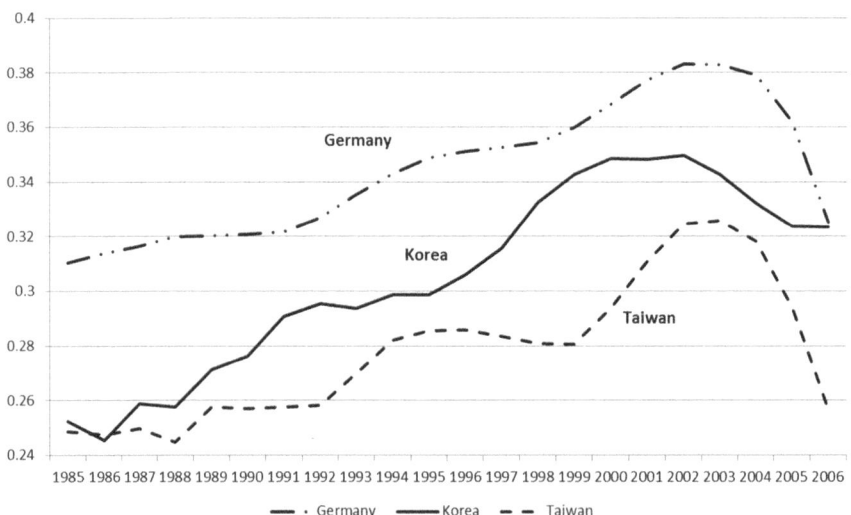

Fig. 5.4 Originality in selected countries. *Note* Originality is calculated with following formula: $1 - \sum_{k=1}^{N_i} S_{ik}^2$, where k is the technological class, and S_{ik} is the percentage of citations made by patent i to patents belonging to patent class k, out of N_i patent classes. Higher value of originality means the patents relies for invention on other patents from a wider range of technological fields. *Source* Statistical data from Lee (2013)

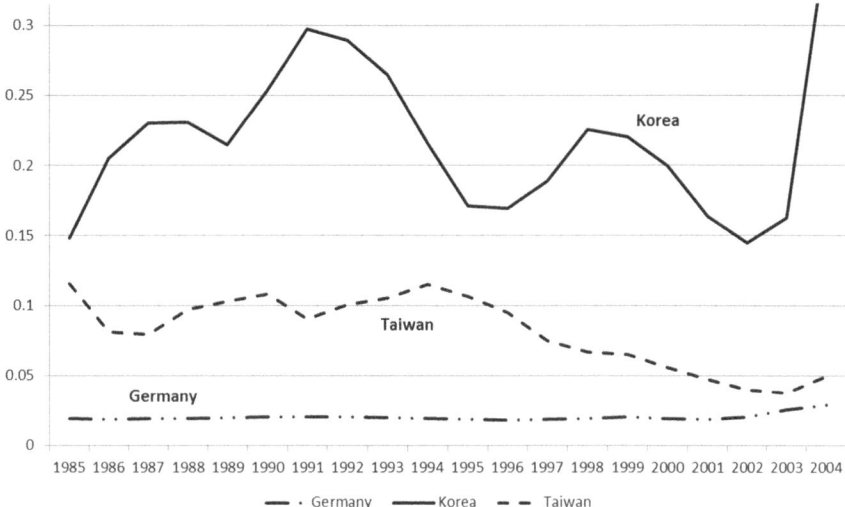

Fig. 5.5 Concentration of inventors in selected countries. *Note* Concentration of inventors is measured with following formula using the Herfindahl-Hirschman index: $\sum_{i \in I_x} \left(\frac{N_{it}}{N_{xt}^*} \right)^2$, where I_x is the set of assignees, N_{it} is the number of patents filed by assignee i in year t, and N_{xt}^* is the total number of patents filed by country x in year t excluding unassigned patents. It ranges from zero to one, and high value means that patents are filed and owned by a few number of agents, while low value means that applications are made by a large number of diverse inventors. *Source* Statistical data from Lee (2013)

main inventors of knowledge creation in South Korea are a few big businesses with a tendency not to interact with each other, leading to low mutual citations. Taiwan, on the hand, has a high level of mutual citations among its small and medium-sized enterprises which are in close interaction with each other.

As shown in Lee (2013), one of the most noticeable aspects of the NIS in a typical advanced country in contrast to the case of NIS in the catch-up stage, is that it tends to show a pattern of specialization in technologies with a long cycle time, a high degree of localization in knowledge creation, a low degree of concentration, and a high level of technological diversification. This implies that when the catching-up is completed or the post-catching-up stage is reached, countries previously following the catching-up model need to switch to sectors with longer cycle times of technology as well as to diversify technology and inventor portfolios and raise the degree of localization of knowledge creation. This is because economic growth in high-income economies is significantly related to specializing in technologies with longer cycle times (e.g. pharmaceuticals, biotechnology, and materials), a higher degree of localization of knowledge, and an even distribution of inventors (less concentration), as shown by regressions in Lee (2013, Chap. 3).

To sum up, in order to make a transition to the NIS resembling a top-tier advanced country like Germany, South Korea needs to lower the excessive degree

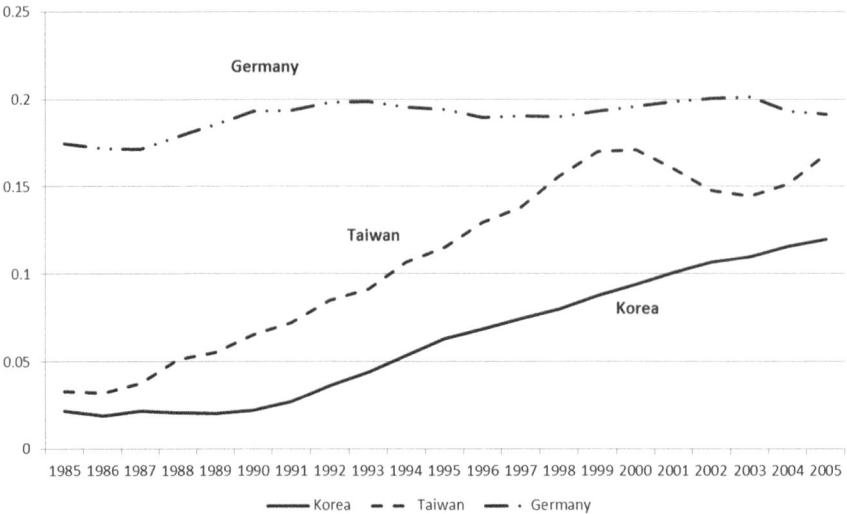

Fig. 5.6 Localization of knowledge creation in selected countries. *Note* Localization of knowledge creation is the normalized self-citation ratio at the country level. This is calculated with following formula: $\frac{n_{xxt}}{n_{xt}} - \frac{n_{cxt}}{n_{ct}}$, where n_{xxt} is the number of citations made to country x's patents by country x's patents filed in year t (self-citation ratio), n_{xt} is the number of total citations made by country x's patents filed in year t, n_{cxt} is the number of citations made to country x's patents by all patents except country x's patents filed in year t, and n_{ct} is the number of total citations made by all patents filed in year t except country x's patents. Higher value of this indicator means that a country relies more on domestically-owned technologies (or patents owned by same-nationality inventors) than on foreign-owned technologies. *Source* Statistical data from Lee (2013)

of concentration, raise the degree of localization of knowledge creation and technological diversification, and speed up the transition process to specialize in sectors with longer cycle times of technology, which has already begun.

5.5 Policy Implication: Reforming the NIS in Korea

So far, the analysis has shown that South Korea passed through the first technological turning point after the mid-1980s by specializing in and entering sectors with short cycle times of technology. The country has thus been very successful in catching up to the income level of advanced countries. At the same time, South Korea also achieved a certain degree of localization in knowledge creation and technological diversification. Since the 2000s, South Korean government has promoted industries such as biotechnology. As a result, South Korea was able to pass through the second technological turning point by entering sectors with longer cycle times of technology, but this is still an ongoing process. Although such industrial promotion policy succeeded in producing a certain number of patents (knowledge), it is generally agreed that those industries have not yet achieved commercial success.

There are potential doubts about the necessity of entering into industries with longer cycle times of technology, which are usually difficult for latecomers to succeed in due to high entry barriers and a long gestation period. Instead, one might suggest that South Korea should continue specializing in sectors with shorter cycle times of technology (such as IT) in which it is performing very well. However, the problem is that as South Korea has successfully caught up in sectors with shorter cycle times of technology, other developing countries such as China could also quickly and easily catch up with Korea in those industries within a short period of time. China is currently catching up the fastest in sectors with shorter cycle times of technology such as cell phones, while the catching-up speed for industries such as automobile, machine parts and source materials is relatively slow.

Therefore, one may reason that only if South Korea successfully enters sectors with longer cycle times of technology and high entry barriers would the country be able to achieve sustainable economic growth with less worry about China's catching up. Therefore, South Korea needs to continuously enter sectors such as renewable energy industries (solar, wind, tidal and geothermal energy), medical products including bio-similar which Samsung has recently been targeting, and bioplastics or 'white bio' which is considered less difficult to enter than the so-called 'green bio' (organic foods).

Leaping into sectors with long cycle times of technology is not the only problem South Korea faces. As shown by the analysis in the preceding section on NIS, the country also needs to raise the degree of localization of knowledge creation and technological diversification, and lower the excessive degree of concentration. However, it will be very difficult to make this transition with the current NIS led by big businesses. Instead, the participation of various agents such as small and medium enterprises is required. This is why it is necessary to shift from the imbalanced catching-up strategy to the balanced co-catching-up strategy.

We can also suggest some policy ideas to promote the so-called 'creative economy' which has become the slogan of the Park government since 2013. Schumpeter (1934: 65) stressed that creation is not making something totally new from nothing, but rather making new combinations from existing objects. This idea of creation as a new combination is the appropriate way to promote a creative economy. That is, it would be very difficult to find something completely new. Instead, one needs to combine existing things to create new economic engines. In this light, we can suggest pursuing three types of new combinations.

First, as mentioned above, in order to lower the excessive degree of concentration across inventors, there should be a new combination of big businesses and SMEs (new combination 1). This would enable the SMEs to produce more knowledge (patents), but does not mean that big businesses which have led economic growth in the past should be suppressed. It means creating a new constructive relationship between big businesses and SMEs. Second, there should be a new combination of labor and management, so that firms may reduce working hours and raise productivity (new combination 2). This would help in raising the degree of localization of knowledge creation because it would diversify and localize the source of innovation from elite scientists in big businesses to engineers and workers in SMEs. It would also mean new combinations of explicit knowledge from elite scientists and tacit knowledge from onsite engineers and workers. Third, new combination 3 regards the fusion of a variety of technologies in diverse fields to create new knowledge, which implies improvement in technological diversification. For example, South Korea could combine IT with BT (biotechnology) and NT (nanotechnology). Given the strength of South Korea in IT, this could open new business areas and create new business models.

Overall, this chapter argues that South Korea needs to overcome three weaknesses in the current NIS (high degree of concentration, low degree of knowledge localization and narrow technological diversification) through three new combinations: a new combination of big and small firms, a new combination of labor and management, and a new combination of technologies.

References

Acemoglu D, Robinson JA (2012) Why nations fail. Crown Business, New York
Jaffe AB, Trajtenberg M (2002) Patents, citations, and innovations: a window on the knowledge economy. MIT Press, Cambridge
Jaffe AB, Trajtenberg M, Forgaty MS (2000) Knowledge spillovers and patent citations: evidence from a survey of inventors. Am Econ Rev 90(2):215–218
Jaffe AB, Trajtenberg M, Henderson R (1993) Geographic localization of knowledge spillovers as evidenced by patent citations. Quart J Econ 108(3):577–598
Lee K (2013) Schumpeterian analysis of economic catch-up: knowledge, path-creation, and the middle-income trap. Cambridge University Press, Cambridge
Lee K, Kim BY (2009) Both institutions and policies matter but differently for different income groups of countries: determinants of long-run economic growth revisited. World Dev 37(3):533–549
Lee K, Kim YK (2010) IPR and technological catch-up in Korea. In: Odagiri H, Goto A, Sunami A, Nelson RR (eds) Intellectual property rights, development, and catch up: an international comparative study. Oxford University Press, Oxford, pp 133–162
Lee K, Yoon M (2010) International, intra-national, and inter-firm knowledge diffusion and technological catch-up: the USA, Japan, Korea, and Taiwan in the memory chip industry. Technol Anal Strateg Manag 22(5):553–570
Lee YH et al (2014) Hangukhyong Sijang Gyoungjae Chaejae (Korean-style market economy system). SNU Press, Seoul (in Korean)
Lundvall B (1992) National systems of innovation: toward a theory of innovation and interactive learning. Pinter Publishers, London
Park K, Lee K (2006) Linking the technological regimes to the technological catch-up: analyzing Korea and Taiwan using the US patent data. Ind Corp Change 15(4):715–753
Schumpeter JA (1934) Theory of economic development: an inquiry into profits, capital, credit, interest, and the business cycle. Harvard University Press, Massachusetts
World Bank (2010) Escaping the middle-income trap. In World Bank East Asia Pacific economic update: robust recovery, rising risks, vol 2. World Bank, Washington, D.C.

Chapter 6
From the Developmental to the Universal Welfare State: Lost in Transition?

Huck-ju Kwon

6.1   Introduction

For the last six decades, Korea has been able to establish a comprehensive welfare system from a minimal number of programs together with economic development and democratic consolidation. It is a remarkable achievement and provides very useful policy lessons to many developing countries which aspire to escape the predicament of underdevelopment. While such achievements are commendable, Korea is now faced with difficult challenges to consolidate its position and move to the next level of development. In terms of economic growth, the Korean economy has been encroached by the advance of other developing countries such as China and Vietnam, while it has not been able to match the competitive edge of the US and Japanese economies. Ordinary citizens are now more exposed to social risks such as precarious employment, and family and work imbalance due to labor market reforms since the East Asian economic crisis. A demographic shift due to longevity and low fertility has also created new demand for social services like long-term care for the elderly and child-care. At the same time, a large proportion of the population is still outside of the core programs of social policy such as public pensions and unemployment insurance programs. A transition from the developmental welfare state to the universal welfare state is the next challenge for Korea in social protection.

Indeed, there have been a series of political debates about the universal welfare state for some time, in particular since the presidential election in December 2012. The two leading candidates in the tight election pledged that they would strengthen the welfare state once they were in government. The eventual winner, Park Geun-hye, promised that her government would make social welfare top priority for public policy, while the opposition candidate promised a universal welfare state in

H. Kwon (✉)
Graduate School of Public Administration, Seoul National University, Seoul, South Korea
e-mail: hkwon4@snu.ac.kr

© Springer International Publishing AG 2017   83
J. Choi et al. (eds.), *The Korean Government and Public Policies in a Development Nexus*, The Political Economy of the Asia Pacific, DOI 10.1007/978-3-319-52473-3_6

which everyone could be protected by social policy programs. What emerged from the debate during the presidential election was a strong social consensus among politicians and the public alike that Korea should reform the developmental welfare state and turn to a universal welfare state. What is the underlying social and economic background for such consensus? What are the policy programs that have been introduced for this purpose? Is the universal welfare state a realistic possibility in Korea? In this Chapter, we will examine the policy efforts for universal welfare against the background of the demographic shift and labor market change in Korea, and seek to answer the question of whether such effort will lead to a universal welfare state.

In the next section, this Chapter will first discuss the reform of the developmental welfare state in the wake of the Asian economic crisis, and argue that it became more inclusive than in the previous period. In the following section, we will discuss the demographic shift and labor market changes that have created new social risks and created a social need for a universal welfare state. In Sect. 6.4 we will trace the political debates on the universal welfare state. We will also elaborate further the notion of the universal welfare state in contrast to the developmental welfare state and elaborate what is meant by a transition to the universal welfare state. In Sect. 6.5, we will examine social policies under the Park Geun-hye government and try to answer the question of whether they will lead to a universal welfare state.

6.2   Reform of the Developmental Welfare State

The welfare system in Korea has many distinctive characteristics, which can be well captured by the notion of the developmental welfare state (Kwon 2005). The developmental welfare state essentially refers to a policy arrangement of social welfare in which social programs are primarily utilized as instruments for economic development while social protection for citizens is relegated to the secondary concern for social policy (Goodman and White 1998). In fact, social policy programs did indeed prove a highly effective policy instrument during the period of rapid economic development. Industrial Accident Insurance introduced in 1963, the Civil Service Pension in 1961, and the National Health Insurance in 1977 were set to protect those workers and bureaucrats who were considered as strategic for economic development. The obvious downside of the developmental welfare state was to leave the vulnerable section of the population such as the poor, elderly and children virtually outside of the welfare state. People working in informal sectors such as vendors in street markets and workers in small business were also left out of the welfare state. The role of the state in welfare was mainly that of regulator in which the state regulated social and economic agencies to provide and finance social welfare (Kwon 1997). Through this arrangement, the state could minimize social spending while putting a greater portion of financial resources toward economic development.

The justification for the rationale of 'economy-first' was that it was temporal in nature. A poor and war-torn country like Korea should devote its resources and energy to economic development and the social protection programs were introduced first for those who could contribute to such endeavors (Adelman 1997). Once economic development picked up the pace, social policy could be extended to the wider section of the population. Indeed, National Health Insurance was gradually but swiftly expanded through the 1980s, and able to cover the entire population by 1988. It was first implemented to cover those who worked in large scale industries in 1977, but was extended to those working in smaller firms in the 1980s. In 1988, the public health insurance program was extended to cover farmers, informal sector workers, and other people without employment status as residence-based members. Industrial accident insurance was extended its coverage from large to small scale firms during the 1960s and 1970s. Nevertheless, other social policies such as public pension programs remained workplace-based, covering mainly those with employment status such as civil servants, school teachers, and military personnel. Although the National Pension Program was extended during the late 1980s, it does not yet cover the entire working population.

Despite the selective nature of the developmental welfare state, inequality was kept at a relatively low level during the period of rapid economic growth (Kwon 1998). It was partly because the rapid expansion of mass education allowed most of the population to participate in the main stream of economic development and partly because the Korean government utilized policy instruments such public health centers, rural cooperatives and vocational schools for social purposes. Most importantly, the land reform implemented from 1946 to 1955 set out the social structure at the macro-level in which rapid economic development could be combined with relative social equality (Cho 2003). Through the land reform, peasants were able to buy a small piece of land at affordable prices, equivalent to a three-year yield. Land holding was limited to small properties for actual farming and only those farming could own agricultural land; large-scale absentee ownership was mostly abolished. The land reform effectively brought an end to the landowning class and created an equal society of small but self-owning farmers. It became a social basis for the mass expansion of education in the 1950s and 60s. Children of peasants would otherwise work in the paddy fields, but they were able to go to schools. They then became a huge army of well-educated and disciplined workers for rapid industrialization in the 1960s and 1970s. It also created the space for autonomy of the state, which would have been constrained by the landowning class (Kwon and Yi 2009). The land reform was a great social policy for social change.

However, the magic combination of economic growth and low social spending could only work so long as economic growth continued. The democratization in the late 1980s gave opportunities to the working class to voice their economic and social demands, which in turn led to a sharp rise in wages. In the late 1990s, Korean firms were faced with economic difficulties, especially higher cost and low productivity. It was identified that the rigid labor market structure had prevented a productivity increase (Park 2001). The government was not able to push forward the necessary labor market and other social reforms due to opposition from political parties and trade unions. The Asian economic crisis, however, forced Korean society to accept such reforms.

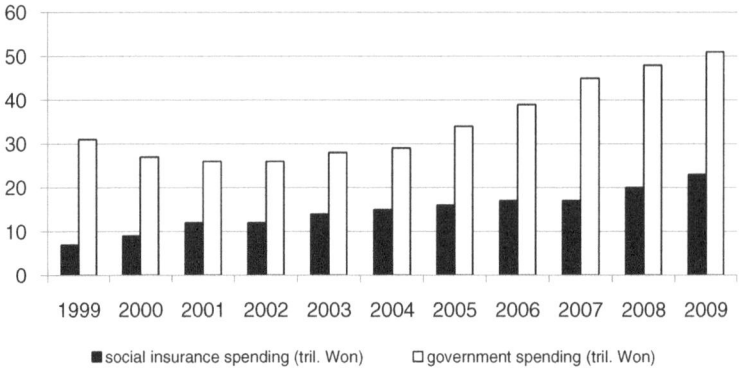

Fig. 6.1 Public spending on social protection in Korea. *Source* Statistics Korea (http://kosis.kr)

The Kim Dae-jung government established a tripartite committee and produced a broad-based social consensus for economic reform, including the labor market reform which would make it easier to lay off workers and to hire temporary workers. In return, the government implemented new social policy programs such as the Minimum Living Standard Guarantee, replacing the meager public assistance for the poor, and extended the Employment Insurance Program to give unemployment benefits to laid-off workers. National Health Insurance was also reformed to cover the entire population under one administrative and financial pooling.

The social policy reform under the Kim Dae-jung government brought a new idea of social rights to the rationale of the welfare state. In particular, the Minimum Living Standard Guarantee introduced by the reform provides poor households with cash and in-kind benefits equal to the minimum living standard as a matter of social right and not a relief stigma as was attached to previous programs. Despite the changes in the programs and the new idea of social welfare, the Korean welfare state maintained the characteristics of the developmental welfare state. First, welfare reform was carried out to facilitate the labor market reform, in particular with respect to the Minimum Living Standard Guarantee and Employment Insurance Program. Second, human capital investment such as training and capacity development was an important rationale for social policy programs. The welfare state reform was dictated to meet policy demands of economic consideration. Figure 6.1 shows the steady increase in public spending on social protection since the late 1990s, which reached more than 10% of GDP in 2009.

6.3   Social and Economic Changes and New Social Risks

Despite the reinforcement of the welfare state, Korean society has been faced with new social risks due to a demographic shift and labor market change. First, demographic ageing has taken place very rapidly in Korea. It is true that Korea

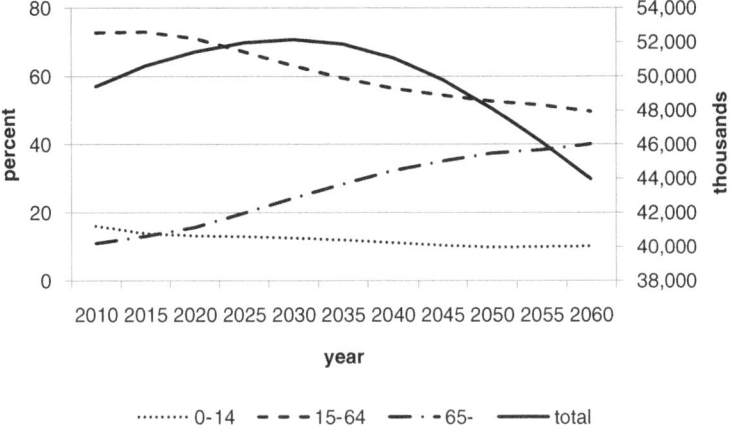

Fig. 6.2 Demographic structure in Korea. *Source* Statistics Korea (http://kosis.kr)

enjoyed a demographic gift, the inflow of the working population, during the rapid economic development in the 1970s and 1980s. The baby-boom generation born after the Korean War gave a double boost to the economy with higher productivity in large numbers. It seems that the Korean population will grow until the late 2010s, but people in the baby-boom generation have already begun to reach old age. Figure 6.2 shows that the elderly population aged over 65 accounted for well over 10% in 2010, 12% in 2015 and a predicted 20% in the near future. Meanwhile the size of the working population has been in steady decline and will be less than 70% in 2025. Such rapid ageing is partly due to the extension of life expectancy for the last six decades. After the Korean War, the life expectancy in Korea was less than 55 years old, but it is now more than 80 years. The rapid ageing is also due to the low fertility late, which is the lowest in the world.

The demographic shift will have a strong impact on the economic potential of Korean society, but it also has significant implications for social protection. First, demand from the elderly population for social protection will increase. The number of pensioners will rise sharply and put pressure on the pension fund. Regarding health care, health expenditure will inevitably increase as the growing number of elderly will use health care services, which will probably be much more expensive than before. The long-term care insurance, which was introduced in 2008, will be more utilized as the frail elderly population also increases.

Second, there will be more demand for child-care service although the number of children is in decline. Families with small children will demand child-care services since their ability and willingness to care for children at home will be lower than ever before due to the changing family structure. The government also sees a need for more child-care facilities as it tries to induce young people to form families and to have more children in order to reverse the decline of the fertility rate. At the same time, the government wants to raise women's labor market participation, which stagnated at around 60.3% in 2015.

Together with the demographic shift, labor market changes have had strong implications for social protection. In the wake of the Asian economic crisis of 1997–98, the Kim Dae-jung government carried out the labor market reform which allowed firms to employ workers on short-term contracts and to use workers dispatched by other agencies. Through this reform, the labor market became more flexible and firms had more room to manage their workforce. Employment, especially with non-regular contracts, also became more precarious. In 2008, the National Assembly passed a new law which obliged employers to give regular contracts to workers with non-regular contracts if they had worked for the same companies in the previous two years. The law was intended to protect the non-regular workers and to reduce the proportion of non-regular workers. The proportion of workers with non-regular contracts has been in decline, though not sharply, over the last few years. There has been, however, a tendency for employers to terminate the contract after two years in order to avoid giving regular contracts to those with previously non-regular contracts. It is still unclear whether the new law limiting the renewal of non-regular contracts has indeed protected non-regular workers better than before (Table 6.1).

These flexible labor reforms, however, have resulted in a dual labor market structure in which there are two clear categories of workers with distinctive characteristics. In terms of wages, the average for non-regular workers is only 56% of what regular workers make overall. Because the wage average does not take into consideration working hours or worker qualifications and other working conditions, the wage differential appears larger than the reality. If one controls for factors such as gender, age, education and marital status, 11% of the wage gap can be accounted for by employment status (National Statistical Office 2014). In terms of the duration of employment in the same firms, regular workers remain in the job for seven years and one month on average, while non-regular workers remain for two years and seven months. In short, regular workers are paid higher and remain longer in the position than workers with non-regular contract.

In terms of social protection, most regular workers are covered by social insurance programs through their workplace. In contrast, only a small portion of the workers with non-regular contracts are covered by social insurance programs. Table 6.2 shows that more than 80% of the workers with regular contracts are included in the National Pension Program, National Health Insurance and the Employment Insurance Program through their workplaces. In other words, the firms

Table 6.1 Regular and non-regular workers by employment status

	2007	2008	2009	2010	2011	2012	2013	2014
Regular workers	15,731	15,932	16,076	16,617	17,065	17,421	17,743	18,397
Non-regular workers	5773	5638	5374	5498	5771	5809	5732	5911
% of non-regular workers	36.7	35.2	33.4	33.1	33.8	33.3	32.3	32.1

Source National Statistical Office (2014)

Table 6.2 Social insurance coverage by employment status (in %)

	National Pension Program (2013)	National Health Insurance	Employment Insurance
Regular workers	82.0	83.9	81.5
Non-regular workers	39.7	46.2	44.0
Average (all)	68.4	71.8	68.6

Source National Statistical Office (2014)

and their employers pay their contributions to the programs so that they will be eligible for benefits once they are in need. In contrast, among those with non-regular contracts, people who are covered by social insurance programs through their workplaces account for only about 40%. Regarding National Health Insurance, they may join the scheme through their local communities, but with respect to the Employment Insurance Program and the National Pension Program, it is very unlikely for them to be included in the programs through their local communities.

All in all, there is a clear dual labor market structure in which one group of people has better pay, job security and social protection while the other group has low pay, precarious employment and less social protection. This is not the society that many Koreans envisioned when they committed themselves to development efforts since the 1960s. The famous catch-phrases 'economy-first' and 'social-welfare later' put forward to the people during the period of rapid economic growth was a kind of social contract that the welfare state would protect everyone once Korean society became affluent. Because of the social fragmentation and inequality emerging in the 2000s, there was a strong undercurrent of grievance about social fragmentation, which then surfaced in the run-up to the presidential election. All the presidential candidates made political promises to the public that their government would build a universal welfare state.

6.4 Searching for the Universal Welfare State

Before we look into the political debate which took place in the presidential election in December 2012, it is necessary to define what the universal welfare state means in the Korean context. In the Korean usage, the welfare state often refers to two different but related meanings. First, it is an ideal society where a high level of well-being is guaranteed for every citizen. It is often seen as the embodiment of a good society. For instance, the Chun Doo-hwan government (in office from 1980 to 1987) launched a political manifesto based on the sentiment: 'Let's Construct a Welfare State' (*Pokchi Kukka Konsôl Hacha*). It was an expression of political intention that his government would enhance the quality of life for Korean people and that society would eventually become a welfare state. President Chun, who took power through a military coup d'état in 1980, wanted to show his commitment to the well-being of ordinary citizens as the justification of his power.

Second, the welfare state simply means a set of institutions and public policies that are intended to protect citizens against social risks. It is a descriptive term rather than a term of value judgment. As an increasing number of social policies and institutions have been introduced over the years, the usage of the welfare state in the second meaning became more widely used than the first. For instance, Kim (2002) published a book entitled, *Debate on the Nature of the Welfare State in Korea* (in Korean) in which the welfare state was used in the second sense. Other authors, including the author of this article, have also used the notion of the welfare state in this sense (Kwon 1999). Because of the two different meanings of welfare state, it might be necessary to qualify the term in order to denote the first meaning of the welfare state, but there was no clear alternative for the time being.

Against the background of the dual labor market structure and subsequent social fragmentation, the debate on the 'universal' welfare state appeared for the first time during the election of the Local Educational Authority in the Kyunggi Province surrounding the Seoul metropolitan area in 2010. Kim Sang-gon, one of the candidates for the head of the Educational Authority, promised that he would provide all school children with free school lunches. At the time of the election, most parents paid fees for lunches for children, and only families with low income were exempt from paying for lunches. Kim Sang-gon explained his idea as follows: "… in the advanced capitalist society, basic welfare should be guaranteed for everyone no matter who gets political power."[1] While there were strong criticisms of his statement in the political establishment, his electoral campaign was a huge success based on the idea of free school meals for all children.

Encouraged by the unexpected electoral success and with an eye on the upcoming general election in April 2012, the main opposition party, the Democratic Party, repeated the welfare initiative with further emphasis on the idea of free welfare services. They promised that their government would make health care free, removing patient co-payments for National Health Insurance. They also pledged to halve the university fee for students. During the general election, however, the 'free-welfare-service' initiatives were not received well by the public and the Democratic Party's electoral return was disappointing. It was seen by the public as a financially unsustainable promise and the Democratic Party was accused by the mainstream media of being reckless. Faced with strong objection, the Democratic Party started to use the term 'universal welfare' instead of 'free welfare'.

In the run-up to the presidential election, welfare issues once again became central to the debates. The leading candidate of the governing party, Park Geun-hye, gave social welfare high policy priority during her campaign. It was an effort to give herself a political identity distinct from the incumbent president, whose standing was in decline. She intended to project herself as a political leader who cares for everyone, not only the well-to-do but also the poor and other weaker

---

[1]Interview with Kim Sang-gon, *Hangyore Daily*, April 2010.

sections of the population. It was also based on political calculation that her welfare initiative would encroach on political support for the opposition party. Social welfare was considered a territory of the Democratic Party. In response, the Democratic Party put forward their promise for the universal welfare state to keep their traditional supporters in the fold. Two major parties were therefore competing with similar welfare promises such as new basic pension allowances for the elderly, extensive child care support and further extension of benefits within National Health Insurance.

In the end, the governing conservative party candidate won the highly competitive presidential election, and it was clear that the universal welfare state emerged as a national consensus, regardless of the winner of the election. Despite the clear consensus, it was not given a clear definition by the political parties. The Democratic Party withdrew their commitment to free health care due to strong criticism, but both parties supported free childcare for families with children under five. Such extension of the welfare state would increase the fiscal burden on the government, but the governing party was not clear about potential tax increases.

It is not difficult to understand why the two major political parties were so keen on making pledges for social welfare. Given the underlying need for social welfare due to the demographic shift toward an ageing society and the fragmentation of the labor market, the political parties tried to mobilize political support by taking advantage of the vulnerability of ordinary citizens. Nevertheless, there were many important questions unanswered about the universal welfare state due to the lack of clear policy rationale. First, the question of financing. Does the universal welfare state provide social welfare for free to everyone, as both the governing and opposition parties promised free childcare services? If it is free for those who receive welfare benefits and services, who will then pay for those benefits? If it is not free, who should pay for benefits and services and who is not obliged to do so? Secondly, the issue of access. Does the universal welfare state provide benefits to everyone? Will there be means-testing in the selection of the beneficiaries of services? Third, the issue of policy priority. Which area of social protection should be given priority: poverty, old-age pension, health care, or childcare?

In order to answer these questions, it is necessary to reflect on the philosophical and normative grounds as well as technical issues of social policy. Elsewhere I have tried to elaborate the idea of the universal welfare state from a normative point of view (Kwon 2014). The justifiable universal welfare state is a public welfare system that provides social protection against social risk for all citizens. Welfare benefits or social services should be given only to those in actual need. At the same time, welfare benefits and social services should be given as a social right. In other words, there should be no stigma attached to people receiving benefits. The level of benefits and quality of social services should match the expectation of the middle class of the society.

In this construction of the universal welfare state, it is important to identify social risks that should be addressed by public policies. Social risks against which the state justifiably protects citizens are two-fold. First at the individual level, we as free and moral persons are obliged to provide protection to fellow citizens against risks that threaten their basic functioning and capabilities as free human beings (Sen 1993). Second at the national level, we are obliged to contribute to efforts that address the social need of the nation as a political and social community, such as educating children to create democratic citizenry and public health services to prevent epidemic diseases (Walzer 1985). These social risks should be addressed to keep the nation in good standing. Both at the individual level and the national level, our efforts to provide social protection to fellow citizens will in turn protect us as free citizens, and this is what we can call the universal welfare state.

In a nutshell, the universal welfare state that we can defend with moral fairness is one that provides universal protection against social risks. Social risks are those that threaten individual functioning and the well-being of the political community. I firmly believe that this kind of universal welfare state will be able to provide a policy rationale for social policy in the future, answering the questions posed above. Nevertheless, this is only one version of a theoretical construction. The practical shape of the universal state is subject to debate in the context of the particular society in question. What should be pointed out during the 2012 presidential election was that political pledges for the universal welfare state were used to mobilize political support, and in consequence they had a strong populist overtone lacking a rigorous conceptual framework as well as financial sustainability.

6.5   Lost in Transition?

Once having taken office, the Park Geun-hye government changed its policy direction to the 'Creative Economy', relegating welfare initiatives to low priority. The Park government's first Minister of Health and Welfare, Chin Young, resigned over the controversy surrounding the new basic pension program in September 2013. Minister Chin insisted on keeping the original plan, in which 70% of the elderly over 65 years of age would receive non-contributory basic pensions of 200,000 KRW (equivalent to 166 USD) per month, but the government wanted to reduce the amount of basic pensions for the elderly receiving pensions from the National Pension Program. In the Regular Session of the National Assembly in October 2013, the revision of the Basic Pension Law was passed to install a pension scheme with a sliding scale in relation to other pension incomes, although there was a strong objection from the opposition party. The result is that some of the elderly will receive a smaller amount of basic pension than was promised. It was a huge policy retreat for the Park government, and showed that the political promise for the universal welfare state was made during the election without careful consideration of financial sustainability.

In 2014, the Park government launched a reform plan for the Civil Service Pension Program. The government's reform proposal was to reduce pensions for retired civil servants in order to make the pension program financially sustainable. The policy option that the government wanted to pursue was a kind of retrenchment reform reducing the level of social security, which the Civil Service Union strongly resisted.

In contrast, the Civil Service Union preferred an increase in contribution so that the level of pension could be maintained alongside the reduction of pensions. Either way, the reduction in pensions or an increase in contribution would make the financing of the Civil Service Pension Program more viable given the steady increase of pensioners over the last couple of decades. Despite the opposition of the Civil Service Union, the government bill was submitted to the National Assembly where a special cross-party commission was established to consider it. After a year of deliberation, the cross-party commission reached a compromise which would increase the level of contributions that civil servants would pay as well as reduce the level of pensions for retired civil servants in May 2015. The compromise sparked an internal conflict between the governing party and the government, and in consequence the leader of the governing party was forced to resign by the president. This episode in the reform of the Civil Service Pension Program indicated that the government policy priority was not social security, but rather financial sustainability.

The universal welfare state seems to have been lost in transition from Park's election campaign to taking government office. The political confrontation in 2015/2016 between the central government and local governments over free childcare services again showed that the universal welfare state has become a political hot potato which is no longer taken seriously. In fact, Park Geun-hye as a presidential candidate promised that all families with children aged under five would be able to use free childcare services, and a pre-school program, which had been implemented for children of low income families since 2012. Since the free childcare program was financed partly by the central government and partly by the local government, many local governments experienced fiscal strain due to the program for the first three years of the Park government. For the financial year 2016, some local governments, especially headed by the politicians of the opposition party, demanded extra financial subsidies from the central government for free childcare services. These local government mayors and governors argued that the free childcare program was a central government responsibility because it was President Park's electoral promise. The central government insisted that the local government should meet their financial responsibility. At the time of writing, this political stalemate continued without a clear path to a solution.

All in all, the new basic pension for 70% of the elderly aged over 65 and free childcare for children under five were policy responses to address new social risks that the demographic shift to an aged society with low fertility has created. They were also conceived from the view point of the universal welfare state. The Park government's retreat regarding basic pensions and political confrontation with the local governments with respect to free childcare services indicated that there was an inadequate vision and plan, if not a complete lack thereof, toward achieving the universal welfare state. This is perhaps not so surprising given that the notion of the universal welfare was hastily and irresponsibly floated without a clear vision and plan during the election. It is not just the government but also the opposition party which adopted a populist campaign about the universal welfare state without a clear financial plan. In terms of plans for policy instruments, existing programs such as the Minimum Living Standard Guarantee and the National Pension Program could be revised to address poverty among the elderly population. At present under the rules of the Minimum Living Standard Guarantee, poor elderly families with working age children are not eligible for income support regardless of whether or not the children provide income support for elderly parents. The introduction of new basic pensions should have been made with a more careful consideration in relation to the revision of the Minimum Living Standard Guarantee.

Regarding childcare, the government created an abrupt increase in demand for childcare services through the extension of free childcare to all children under five. Public facilities fell short of demand, and the provision of childcare by private institutions sharply increased. There have been many complaints about the low quality of care from private providers. It was also necessary to assess whether the local governments would be able to sustain the fiscal burden of the services. After three years of implementation, a political confrontation over financing free child-care took place between the central and local governments due to the fiscal pressure on the local governments. In the middle of the political disputes, parents of small children were left in an awkward situation not knowing whether they would be able to send their children to nurseries.

While these new programs were introduced by the Park government, the main programs of the welfare state still leave a great deal of the population without adequate protection. Table 6.3 shows that public pension programs including the National Pension Program, the Civil Service Pension, the School Teacher Pension and the Military Personnel Pension Program cover 50.7% of the target population while the rest are left outside of the programs for various reasons such as non-paying contributions or economic inactivity. With respect to the Employment Insurance Program, 43.2% of employed persons currently pay contributions to the program so that they will be eligible for unemployment benefits if they are unemployed. Those outside the program, 56.7%, would receive no unemployment benefits, even if they became unemployed. The Minimum Living Standard Guarantee also provides only 57.1% of poor persons with income support, while the rest of the poor are not eligible because they have family members who should theoretically be supporting them. These three programs together with National Health Insurance are the core contours of the welfare state in Korea, but the fact that they currently cover only about the half of the target population indicates that Korean society is still far away from establishing a universal welfare state. It also suggests that there is no clear strategy to reach this aim through, for example, setting policy priorities.

Table 6.3 The coverage of three main social policy programs (in %)

Programs	Target population	Covered	Not covered
Public Pensions	Working age population	50.7	49.3
Employment Insurance Program	Employed persons	43.2	56.7
Min. Living Standard Guarantee	Poor persons	57.1	42.8

Sources National Pension Corporation (2015), Ministry of Health and Welfare (2014)

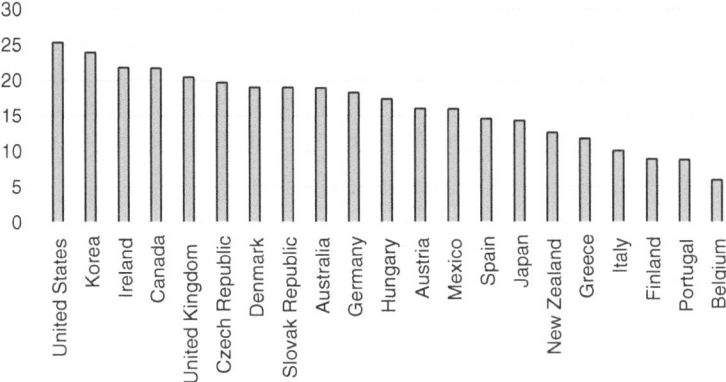

Fig. 6.3 International comparison of the low income workers. *Source* OECD data (Wages and Earnings)

Another sign that the universal welfare state is not on the government agenda is the labor market reform, which the Park government tried to implement in 2015. This chapter has highlighted that there is a clear dual labor market structure in the Korean economy, divided into employees with regular contracts and employees with non-regular contracts. There is an obvious demarcation line between those with regular contracts and those with non-regular contracts in terms of the level of pay, job security and social protection. The dual labor market structure has pressed down wages, especially for low-end wage earners. According to OECD statistics (see Fig. 6.3), the Korean economy, together with the US economy, has the highest proportion of low wage workers, which is defined as less than two-thirds of the median wage. To address such a dual structure in the labor market, the Park government proposed a reform that would make is easier for firms with regular workers to justify lay-offs. Under the reform, firms can carry out performance evaluations of their employees and, according to evaluation outcomes, will be able to lay off the so-called low performing employees.

This reform proposal aims to give firms more flexibility in managing employees, but the regular workers who have been in more secure job situations than non-regular workers will be put in more precarious positions. The reform package also includes a provision that would allow firms to renew non-regular contracts after two years of employment without upgrading the contracts to regular ones. This provision was intended to reduce the practice of not renewing contracts for non-regular workers in order to avoid the rigidity that regular employment would bring about. The Korean Trade Union Congress strongly opposed the reform, arguing that the reform would encourage a race-to-the-bottom in the labor market. The tripartite committee of the government, business and trade unions, tried to find some form of compromise in 2015, but failed to do so.

In the National Assembly, the government was unable to persuade the opposition parties to pass the labor market reform bill. The procedural rule in the National Assembly prevented the governing party from putting the bill up for vote without a concession of the opposition party. With the general election looming large, it seems unlikely that the government will push through the labor market reform bill.

6.6 Conclusion

Through the extension of social policy programs in the wake of the Asian economic crisis, the developmental welfare state became more inclusive. This chapter, however, has pointed out that the developmental welfare state with a more inclusive profile cannot effectively deal with the new social risks which have emerged in Korea since the 2000s. The demographic shift toward an aged society with very low fertility and the dual labor market structure have created new social risks which the developmental welfare state could not effectively address. The notion of the universal welfare state was brought to public debate in response to the new social risks, especially during the presidential election at the end of 2012.

The ideal of the universal welfare state, where every citizen is guaranteed access to social protection, was not just a response to current social need. This chapter shows that the developmental welfare state, which was arranged in order to support economic development, was temporal in nature. Each program such as National Health Insurance and the National Pension Program were all set to be universal and to include everyone in need. The catch-phrase 'economy-first', made famous by President Park Chung-hee during the period of rapid economic development, also implicitly assumed that the welfare state for every citizen would become a reality once Korea becomes an affluent society.

Against such a historical and social background, the universal welfare state was promised by most of the mainstream political parties and their presidential candidates during the election. In this chapter, it is made clear that there was a strong populist overtone without careful consideration of the viability of policy programs and their financial sustainability. This has clearly manifested in the policy retreat by the Park Geun-hye government in relation to the new basic pensions. The central and local governments have been locked into political confrontation in relation to free childcare services.

Once taking office, the Park government placed a strong emphasis on policy for a 'creative' economy rather than a universal welfare state. Her main reform program was the retrenchment of the Civil Service Pension Program and the labor market reform which would bring flexibility surrounding workers with regular contracts. The labor reform programs would increase precariousness in employment for regular workers without enhancing social security for those with non-regular contracts. Despite the policy reversal of the Park government, there will be a strong need for a universal welfare state due to continued social and demographic changes.

The universal welfare state promised by politicians including President Park Geun-hye during the election may be a false dawn, and the labor market reform which the government has pursued would lead to further insecurity. Nevertheless, due to the social and demographic shift experienced by Korean society as well as political demand, the universal welfare state will be inevitable sooner or later. In order to make a successful transition from a developmental welfare state to a universal welfare state, it will be necessary to shape such a universal welfare state in a way compatible with economic development. At the same time, it will be necessary to construct the universal welfare state as morally fair and acceptable to all citizens. This will be an important task for the sustainable progress of Korean society.

References

Adelman I (1997) Social development in Korea, 1953–1993. In: Cha D, Kim K, Perkins D (eds) The Korean economy 1945–1995. Korea Development Institute, Seoul, pp 509–540

Cho S (2003) Land reform and capitalism in Korea. In Yoo C (ed) The history of the Korean development model and its crisis. Cobook, Seoul (in Korean)

Goodman R, White G (1998) Welfare orientalism and the search for an East Asian welfare model. In: Goodman R, White G, Kwon HJ (eds) The East Asian welfare model: welfare orientalism and the state. Routledge, London

Kim Y (ed) (2002) Debates on the nature of the welfare state in Korea. Human-being and Welfare, Seoul (in Korean)

Kwon H (1997) Beyond European welfare regimes: comparative perspectives on East Asian welfare systems. J Soc Policy 26(4):467–484

Kwon H (1999) The welfare state in Korea: the politics of legitimation. Macmillan, London

Kwon H (2005) Transforming the developmental welfare state in East Asia. Dev Change 36 (3):477–497

Kwon H (2014) Searching for normative grounds of the universal welfare state: transition of the developmental welfare state in Korea

Kwon H, Yi I (2009) Economic development and poverty reduction in Korea: governing multifunctional institutions. Dev Change 40(4):769–792

Kwon S (1998) The Korean experience of poverty reduction: lessons and prospects. In: KDI/UNDP (ed) Poverty alleviation. Korea Development Institute, Seoul

Ministry of Health and Welfare (2014) White paper on Health and Welfare: Ministry of Health and Welfare (in Korean)

National Pension Corporation (2015) The coverage of Public Pension Programmes National Pension Corporation. National Pension Corporation, Seoul (in Korean)

National Statistical Office (2014) Extra survey on employment status. National Statistical Office, Seoul (in Korean)

Park B (2001) Labor regulation and economic change: a view on the Korean economic crisis. Geoforum 32(1):61–75

Sen A (1993) Capability and well-being. In: Nussbaum MC, Sen A (eds) The quality of life. Oxford University Press, Oxford

Walzer M (1985) Spheres of justice: a defence of pluralism and equality. Blackwell, Oxford

Chapter 7
South Korea's Policy Responses to the Changing Trade Environment in the Post-Uruguay Round Period

Min Gyo Koo

7.1 Introduction

South Korea is considered one of the most successful countries in post-war economic development history and is often dubbed the "miracle on the Han River." At the end of 2011, it joined the "one-trillion-dollar trading club," departing from the ranks of newly emerging countries to become the ninth largest trading country in the world. After reaching the $100 million mark in 1964, South Korea's exports grew more than five thousand times in less than five decades, making it the seventh-largest exporting country (Koo 2013: 95).

South Korea's growth story, however, was not always full of miracle and wonder. Its growing openness to trade caused or exacerbated many economic and social problems, including the debt crisis in the early 1980s, the financial crisis at the end of the 1990s, and the economic slowdown in the late 2000s, to name a few. The political and economic conditions that had underpinned South Korea's traditional trade policy paradigm came under scrutiny, especially in the second half of the 1990s. The growing pressure for trade liberalization as a result of the Uruguay Round (UR) from 1986 to 93 and the outbreak of the Asian financial crisis in 1997–98 was a painful wake-up call to change the mercantilist trade policy regime based on export promotion and import protection.

South Korea has thus far successfully adapted its trade policy to the competitive pressure of globalization. Instead of letting the market alone determine who will gain and who will lose from greater trade openness, the South Korean government has deliberately and proactively chosen the timing, speed, and scope of trade liberalization. One of the most prominent features of South Korea's policy transformation is its embrace of preferential trading arrangements. South Korea has thus far concluded fifteen free trade agreements (FTAs) with Chile, Singapore, the

M.G. Koo (✉)
Graduate School of Public Administration, Seoul National University, Seoul, South Korea
e-mail: mgkoo@snu.ac.kr

© Springer International Publishing AG 2017   99
J. Choi et al. (eds.), *The Korean Government and Public Policies in a Development Nexus*, The Political Economy of the Asia Pacific,
DOI 10.1007/978-3-319-52473-3_7

European Free Trade Association, the Association of Southeast Asian Nations (ASEAN), the United States, India, Peru, the European Union (EU), Turkey, Colombia, Australia, Canada, China, New Zealand and Vietnam. South Korea's partner selection, if not the total number of signed agreements, has been truly remarkable as the list includes both small and large trading partners across the world (Koo 2009, 2010; Sohn and Koo 2011; Koo and Jho 2013).

At the domestic level, international trade always creates a conflict of interest between workers and capital owners, between urban and rural areas, and between competitive and uncompetitive sectors. In the course of comprehensive trade liberalization through FTAs, the South Korean government provided uncompetitive domestic sectors and factors, which had been largely shielded from international competition, with generous side payments. South Korea's approach proves that state involvement is necessary in mitigating the adverse effects of trade liberalization on the domestic political economy. The South Korean government found that direct cash allowances were particularly effective in pacifying otherwise fierce opposition to greater trade openness.

However, such an ad hoc approach to assistance for trade adjustment is no longer sustainable, not only because trade compensation is increasingly becoming a fiscal burden for the government, but also because South Korea's maturing democracy is demanding greater accountability and transparency in the trade policymaking process. The rise and fall of the Office of the Minister for Trade (OMT) (1998–2013) as a chief trade negotiation agency illustrates the point.

The adjustment and adaptation of South Korea's trade policy to the dual challenge of greater trade openness and democratic governance is still under way. But the time is now ripe to assess South Korea's first twenty years under the new World Trade Organization (WTO) regime. This chapter thus aims to examine South Korea's policy responses to both internal and external challenges in the post-Uruguay Round period. It will highlight why South Korea was intermittently drawn into internal challenges and external crises and how it responded quickly by repositioning, adapting, and restructuring for competitiveness.

Section 7.2 outlines the patterns of trade policy in South Korea and Asian countries more broadly, before and after the conclusion of UR negotiations. This section evaluates the launch of the WTO and its impact on South Korea's trade policy. It is highlighted that South Korea has undergone a dramatic change in terms of trade policy orientation over the past two decades, but primarily in accordance with its obligations and commitments under the WTO.

Section 7.3 examines the changing institutional landscape in Asia in the post-UR period, focusing on the proliferation of preferential trading arrangements. South Korea's position in the global and regional web of FTAs was unique as it remained excluded from preferential arrangements. However, it has successfully concluded many comprehensive FTAs over the past decade. This section explains how such an achievement was made possible and then argues that South Korea's trade policy has shifted from a developmental-mercantilist position to a developmental-but-liberal approach.

Section 7.4 analyzes the origins and evolution of South Korea's developmental liberalism during the Kim Dae-jung and Roh Moo-hyun administrations. Then, this section examines key domestic players and their policy goals, focusing on the rise and fall of the OMT. For the first decade after the International Monetary Fund's (IMF) bailout program for South Korea officially ended in August 2001, OMT-led trade liberalization through FTAs seemed quite successful. Despite domestic concerns about welfare distribution, the OMT success story attracted envy among Asian peer countries including Japan, where trade negotiations were often bogged down by interest group politics and bureaucratic stalemate. However, the sudden demise of the OMT demonstrates the growing demand for greater transparency in and accountability for the kind of rapid trade liberalization that took place in the 2000s. Despite a series of reforms, the governance of trade policymaking and negotiations remains in flux, if not in complete disarray.

Section 7.5 summarizes key arguments and draws policy implications for South Korea's future trade policy and for other developing countries as well. Government-led trade liberalization has helped South Korea to effectively respond to the pressure of globalization for the past two decades. However, such a developmentalist liberal strategy is increasingly becoming incompatible with and unpalatable to South Korea's maturing democracy. This section concludes that any sustainable trade policy should strike a correct balance between democracy and trade openness, and that South Korea will continue to be a benchmark country in this regard.

7.2   Patterns of South Korean Trade

South Korea's remarkable economic takeoff for the past five decades can be best illustrated by the increasing share of the country in global trade flows. In 1965, the total value of trade conducted by South Korea was US$636 million, constituting 0.163% of the world's total trade. Within a matter of five decades, South Korea's share of world merchandise trade increased by almost twenty times, reaching 2.88% in 2014 (see Fig. 7.1).

In 1965, the US, Western European countries, Australia, Japan and New Zealand accounted for about 70% of world merchandise trade. By 2004 these countries accounted for 61%. The reduction is a result of the emergence of Asia as an important producer of exports. However, as Asia was growing in importance as an exporter, Africa and Latin America registered a considerable reduction in their already meager share of world export. Africa's share fell from 5 to 2% while Latin America declined from 7 to 5% (Kennedy and Nicholas 2009: 2). From 1990 to 2010, Asia's global share soared to 30%. In value-added terms, intra-regional trade during the same period also grew on average by more than 10% per year, two times faster than in other parts of the world (International Monetary Fund 2014: 47).

For South Korea as with other Asian countries, the US was one of the most important trading partners, as evidenced by the share of the US in South Korea's total exports at 22.2% in 1993. In recent years, however, the significance of the US

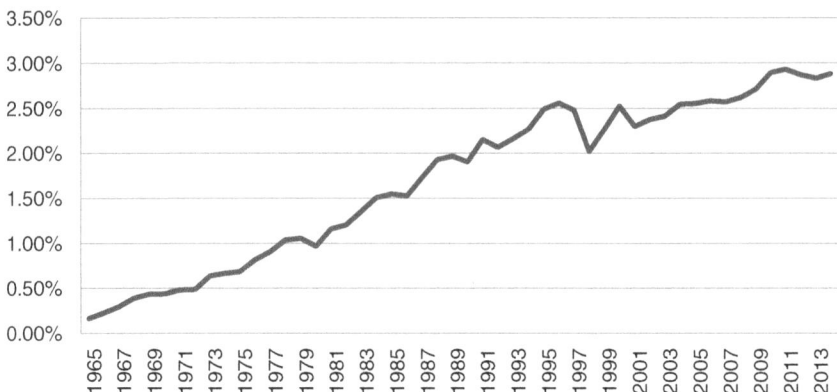

Fig. 7.1 South Korea's share in the world's total merchandise trade. *Source* World Trade Organization Statistics Database (http://stat.wto.org/Home/WSDBHome.aspx?Language=E)

as an export destination for South Korea has been marked by a decrease in its share, falling to 12.3% in 2014. The expanding regional production network centered on China has reduced South Korea's dependence on the US market. In contrast, the share of mainland China in South Korea's total exports has grown rapidly from 6.3% in 1993 to 25.4% in 2014. More notably, China's share of South Korea's total exports is now over 30% if Chinese Hong Kong is included (IMF Direction of Trade Statistics online). The US is an important market for South Korea only as a final destination for exports processed and assembled with intermediate parts in China (Aggarwal and Koo 2016).

In addition to the shifting direction of trade, two features of South Korea's trade pattern are worth noting. First, South Korea's main merchandise exports are manufactured products (86.4% in 2014), while its main imports are raw materials (40.6% in 2014) and manufactured products, including final goods and intermediate parts (52.5%). Second, South Korea's service trade has grown fast over the past decades, amounting to about 20% of merchandise trade (see Table 7.1).

In the meantime, South Korea's tariff policy has been formulated in accordance with its commitments under the WTO. The average *ad valorem* agriculture tariff in 2015 was 49.2%, a slight increase from 47.3% in 1996, partly because of the tariffication of agricultural products under the WTO. The average tariff on manufactured goods was 7.5% in 2015, a slight decrease from 7.7% in 1996. However, South Korea is still criticized for its non-tariff barriers. Since 1995, South Korea has been involved in 683 cases of technical barriers to trade (TBT), the third highest in Asia after China (1082) and Japan (720) in number of cases. Also since 1995, South Korea has been involved in 508 cases of Sanitary and Phytosanitary (SPS) complaints, second in Asia after China (1019 cases) followed by Japan (420 cases) (WTO Integrated Trade Intelligence Portal; I-TIP).

At the broader institutional level, the launch of the WTO in 1995 marked a significant institutional change. Established in 1947, the General Agreement on

Table 7.1   South Korea's trade in goods and services in 2014 (US$ million)

Merchandise trade	Value	Annual percentage change		
	2014	2010–2014	2013	2014
Merchandise *exports*, f.o.b.	572,664	5	2	2
Merchandise *imports*, c.i.f.	525,514	5	−1	2
Breakdown in total exports (%)		**Breakdown in total imports** (%)		
By main commodity group (ITS)		By main commodity group (ITS)		
Agricultural products	2.1	Agricultural products	6.7	
Fuels and mining products	11.2	Fuels and mining products	40.6	
Manufactures	86.4	Manufactures	52.5	
By main destination		By main origin		
1. China	26.1	1. China	16.1	
2. United States	11.1	2. Japan	11.6	
3. European Union (28)	8.8	3. European Union (28)	10.9	
4. Japan	6.2	4. United States	8.1	
5. Hong Kong, China	5.0	5. Saudi Arabia, Kingdom of	7.3	
Commercial services trade	Value	Annual percentage change		
	2014	2010–2014	2013	2014
Commercial services *exports*	105,760	6	0	3
Commercial services *imports*	113,967	4	1	4
Breakdown in total exports (%)		**Breakdown in total imports** (%)		
By principal services item		By principal services item		
Goods-related services	3.3	Goods-related services	7.6	
Transportation	33.4	Transportation	27.7	
Travel	17.2	Travel	20.6	
Other commercial services	46.2	Other commercial services	44.1	

Source World Trade Organization Statistics Database (http://stat.wto.org/Home/WSDBHome.aspx?Language=E)

Tariffs and Trade (GATT) successfully governed national trade policies and global trade flows until the 1970s when a series of economic shocks, particularly two oil crises, caused protectionism in most Western countries. After many successful rounds of multilateral trade negotiations under the auspices of the GATT, the WTO was created in 1995 following the conclusion of the Uruguay Round negotiations.

South Korea joined the GATT in 1967 and became one of the founding members of the WTO. Since its accession to the GATT, South Korea's vigorous promotion of export industries has effectively transformed the once poverty-ridden country into a textbook case of economic development through trade openness. As a resource poor country, South Korea's full integration into the world trading system was inevitable for its economic survival (Koo 2006: 142–143).

However, its position and status between developing and developed countries within the GATT/WTO has been ambivalent until recently. Having been allowed to take fewer obligations and commitments to market openness than richer countries, South Korea enjoyed a developing country status as permitted by its income and general development level at the time of accession to the GATT. Within three decades, however, South Korea became rich enough to join the Organization for Economic Cooperation and Development (OECD) in 1996. Also as a result of the UR, developing countries had to make substantial commitments in a number of areas, including trade in services and intellectual property rights. South Korea's position could no longer be held, although it wanted to extend its claim as much as possible for certain sectors. In the face of growing criticism from Western European countries, South Korea finally graduated from the status of developing country in the late 1990s (Moon and Yoon 2011: 231; Lester et al. 2012).

The 2012 WTO Trade Policy Review (TPR) of South Korea confirmed South Korea's positive progress in liberalization efforts including tariff reductions, concessions in the agricultural sectors, and offers in many services sectors. However, the TPR report also noted that agriculture remained only partly covered by trade agreements, and sensitive agricultural items were excluded from FTA-driven liberalization. In particular, rice was the only item subject to import quotas, which were maintained "mostly for the protection of public morals, human health, hygiene and sanitation, animal and plant life, environmental conservation or essential security interests in compliance with domestic legislation requirements or international commitments" (WTO 2012).[1]

7.3   Institutional Landscape in the Post-UR Period

In 2001, the Doha Development Round was launched in Qatar. From the beginning, it was an uphill battle not only among developed countries but also between developed and developing countries over thorny issues such as agriculture, non-agricultural market access, services, and intellectual property rights. Along with other Asian countries, South Korea had little interest in seeking export markets through preferential trading arrangements until the late 1990s, because the

---

[1]During the UR negotiations, the South Korean government anxiously tried to protect its rice market. As a result, South Korea was allowed to gradually increase its rice import quotas instead of fully opening its rice market under an agreement with the WTO. Eventually, however, the deal expired at the end of 2014 and the South Korean government had to scrap rice-import caps and began to negotiate rice tariff rates with rice exporting countries. It has proposed 513% as an initial rate.

GATT/WTO regime and other informal business networks centered on ethnic ties and alliance relationships provided access to sufficient export markets.[2] At the turn of the new millennium, South Korea was forced to find alternative options. As the new multilateral trade round faltered and resulted in a stalemate, South Korea jumped on the bandwagon of preferential trading arrangements.[3]

The most important locus of trade accords is the active pursuit of bilateral FTAs as well as a web of bilateral FTAs or 'mega-FTAs' (Ravenhill 2001; Pempel 2004, 2010; Aggarwal and Urata 2006; Aggarwal and Koo 2008; Dent 2006; Solís et al. 2009; Aggarwal and Lee 2011).[4] The Japan-Singapore Agreement for New Age Economic Partnership agreed in October 2001 ushered in a series of bilateral FTAs in the following years including agreements between South Korea and Chile (2003), and Japan and Mexico (2004). Also, 'ASEAN+1' agreements proliferated. In February 2003, China signed an FTA framework agreement with the 10 ASEAN countries pledging free trade by 2010, which has now been implemented. Japan followed by starting negotiations of its own in October 2003, but South Korea jumped ahead and signed an FTA with ASEAN in May 2006. As of 2015, the number of Asia-specific FTAs was around 40. If trans-regional accords with countries outside Asia are included, the number rises to over 120 (Aggarwal and Koo 2016: 43).

Concluded by 12 Pacific Rim countries in October 2015, the TPP has become the center of cross-regional trade policy in the Asia-Pacific to rationalize mega-FTAs.[5] In 2009, the US became part of the P4, a grouping created by Singapore, Chile, New Zealand, and Brunei in 2006 which evolved into TPP. President Obama decided to pursue TPP for the reasons below as well as to expand exports to a region that still held significant growth prospects. With Japan's accession to TPP negotiations in

---

[2]In the late 1990s, the network of Japanese multinationals and overseas Chinese businesses played a critical role in creating an informal Asian economic community. American multinational corporations played a similar role in forming a production network in the region, particularly in the electronics sector. Such an informal, "network-style" integration was considered a viable alternative for formal institutionalization of regional trade integration (Encarnation 1999; Katzenstein 2005).

[3]The lament that Asia lacks regional trade institutions has now been replaced by an excessive number of institutional fora that address trade issues wholly or partly in the region. Aside from the WTO, we currently have the ASEAN Free Trade Agreement (AFTA), ASEAN Economic Community (AEC), ASEAN plus 3 (including Japan, China and South Korea), ASEAN plus 8 (or the East Asian Summit, adding India, Australia and New Zealand as well as the US and Russia, most recently), Asia Pacific Economic Cooperation (APEC), and the Trans-Pacific Partnership (TPP) (Aggarwal and Koo 2016: 35).

[4]According to the WTO, 619 notifications of preferential agreements (counting goods, services and accessions separately) were received by the GATT/WTO as of 1 December 2015. Of these, 413 were in force. Currently 278 are officially in force, but the actual number is believed to be higher than the official figures because there are still many accords unreported to the WTO.

[5]Indeed because of this focus on binding rules with few exceptions, the negotiations to conclude TPP have been difficult, with target conclusion dates missed repeatedly before it was eventually signed. The signed agreement faces much more difficult ratification processes in member countries, particularly in the US.

2013, membership expanded to 12 countries. In terms of proposed structure, TPP is likely to be only moderately institutionalized, without a formal organizational structure. But at the same time, given US interests as well as those of the majority of members in creating a genuine architecture that will reign in bilateral FTAs, the outcome is likely to be quite a high degree of hard law, rather than simple proscriptions on behavior (Aggarwal and Koo 2016: 40–41).

In response to the US move toward mega-FTAs, China has also been actively pursuing intra- and cross-regional trade accords. The most important new institutional development endorsed by China centers on the creation of a Regional Comprehensive Economic Partnership (RCEP), which consisted of 16 members and was entering its 11th round of negotiations as of January 2016. In terms of proposed institutional strength, RCEP is likely to remain weak, both in terms of degree of institutionalization and the hardness of rules. RCEP draws on ASEAN's original norms of consensual decision-making and mutual non-interference in member state domestic affairs, but has not become more deeply institutionalized along the lines of ASEAN efforts as noted above. Although RCEP has discussed a wide ranging number of trade issues, it is likely to follow East Asian traditions in containing elements of "sign first" and negotiate later (Aggarwal and Koo 2016: 42–43).

Meanwhile at the APEC summit in Beijing in November 2014, member economies agreed to launch a feasibility study for a Free Trade Area of the Asia-Pacific (FTAAP) as pushed for by the host country, China. This was an idea that had been broached by the US several years ago, but which did not garner much support. However, it will take many years for this proposal to materialize and will thus not likely affect the functioning of the APEC (Aggarwal and Koo 2016: 40).

7.4 South Korean Policy Responses

7.4.1 Changing Policy Preferences and Strategies

In the wake of the Asian financial crisis of 1997–98, as with many other Asian political and business leaders, South Korean leaders held the perception of being forced to accept neoliberal market reforms as prerequisites for Western aid and economic bailout (Dieter 2009: 76). Although the IMF rescue loan program caused region-wide discomfort with the Washington-dominated agency in the late 1990s, South Korea and other crisis-ridden countries in Asia had little choice but to accept the terms and conditions as an instruction manual of neoliberal reform. In addition, there was a 1999 debacle in Seattle where the WTO ministerial meeting failed to launch a new multilateral round of trade talks. It alarmed South Korea's top policymakers that an institutional deadlock in the WTO could severely constrain South Korea's much-needed export market (Koo 2009, 2010, 2013).

The change in policy preferences and strategies was swift and dramatic. In response to the economic crisis, the Kim Dae-jung government (1998–2003) implemented comprehensive reforms effectively swinging South Korea's earlier developmentalist trade policy paradigm in a more liberal direction. Kim's initiative aimed to end a long history of closed-door relations between government officials and business people as symbolized by 'Korea, Inc.' (Lee and Han 2006). It should be noted, however, that the evolution of liberal trade policy still reflected the top-down legacy of the developmental state, with the state playing a critical role in planning, implementing, and monitoring economic reforms (Koo 2010: 111).

In spite of initial opposition from the political and bureaucratic establishment, the Kim administration was more willing than previous administrations to promote competition by applying market discipline to various sectors of the economy. Another development was that market entry and exit became much easier during his presidency (Koo 2009: 186–188). The Kim administration attempted to use foreign competitive pressure to enhance domestic efficiency, as illustrated by the departure from a traditional mercantilist policy toward an active pursuit of FTAs.

The structural changes that followed the Asian financial crisis contributed significantly to a growing belief that preferential liberalization was complementary to multilateral liberalism. In an ironic twist of fate, the unprecedented economic crisis provided the South Korean government with more room for policy autonomy than previously allowed by effectively muffling the country's once rigid protectionist voices (Mo and Moon 1999; Koo 2010).

It became clear that post-crisis external conditions would no longer allow South Korea a free ride in other markets as was usual under the auspices of the GATT/WTO. Kim's reform drive set in motion a significant departure from a mercantilist trade policy platform. Although the linkage between preferential trade liberalization and economic restructuring was not formally stipulated, Kim's turn to FTAs reflected the dualistic nature of his policy ideas: liberal in terms of policy choices (trade liberalization), but fairly top-down and developmental in terms of policy goals (upgrading domestic industries through greater foreign competition) (Koo 2010: 111).[6]

President Roh Moo-hyun (2003–2008) took over Kim's policy initiative by completing the roadmap for FTAs and detailing action plans for a multi-track FTA strategy. Trade liberalization through FTAs became a serious policy bias of the Roh administration. Roh further expanded South Korea's FTA strategy by mobilizing comprehensive side payments to pacify groups which would be negatively affected by trade liberalization (Lee 2006).

There was a growing concern in South Korea's manufacturing sector that the trade deficit would be enlarged as the Korean Won (KRW) had been steadily appreciating since 2001. This undermined the price competitiveness of South Korean manufacturers in the global market. Not only *chaebols* but also small and medium-sized enterprises (SMEs) began to move their production facilities abroad

---

[6]The liberal posture was in clear contrast with generally protectionist attitudes held by most previous administrations in relation to market opening. President Kim Dae-jung was clearly not the first South Korean leader to talk about the country's need for structural reform. Yet the Kim administration stood out for its greater willingness to introduce market discipline to various sectors of the economy that were traditionally protected from competition.

to make up for the disadvantage. Securing export markets through FTAs thus became a top priority to the Roh administration. The Blue House and many trade officials regarded the sacrifice of less competitive sectors, such as agriculture, to be necessary for broader national interests (Koo and Jho 2013: 78).

Such a change in perception was dramatically revealed during negotiations for a South Korea-US FTA (KORUS FTA). At first, the Roh administration's KORUS FTA proposal came as a surprise. In the past, South Korean trade officials took defensive and reactive positions when dealing with their American counterparts. However, South Korean negotiators turned out to be more proactive in completing the most commercially significant FTA for South Korea and the United States since the North American free trade agreement (NAFTA) was concluded in 1993. The negotiation process was certainly not easy, but it took only one year for both parties to sign the landmark deal (Sohn and Koo 2011: 434).[7]

South Korea's decision to negotiate an FTA with the economic superpower can be partly attributed to fear of exclusion from the world's largest market, where South Korea increasingly felt 'sandwiched' between Japan and China both economically and diplomatically. South Korea's top policy elites, particularly in the former Ministry of Foreign Affairs and Trade and the former Ministry of Finance and Economy, believed that preferential access to the US market would not only upgrade South Korea's economic competitiveness by facilitating neoliberal reforms, but also strengthen South Korea's security alliance with the United States (Sohn 2006; Lee and Moon 2008; Sohn and Koo 2011).

In this regard, South Korea's then trade minister, Kim Hyun-chong, was particularly passionate. He tried to instill market discipline in sectors that had been traditionally shielded from international competition. His vision echoed in the Korean developmentalist ambition to depart from the Japanese 'flying geese' model and to find South Korea's future in high-tech and service industries. He hoped that a KORUS FTA would effectively transform the structure of South Korean economy into a more productive American-style liberal economy. Subscribing to this idea, President Roh also became aware of the value of FTAs as diplomatic tools to strengthen strategic ties with South Korea's most important ally, the United States (Sohn and Koo 2011: 445).

The conservative Lee Myung-bak administration (2008–2013) made a series of efforts to abandon the progressive policies of his two predecessors. Trade policy was an exception: the Lee administration adhered to the trade policy agenda set by Presidents Kim and Roh. Despite political turmoil in the first half of 2008 due to controversial US beef imports, the Lee administration continued to pursue the

---

[7]After eight intensive rounds of negotiations beginning in June 2006, South Korea and the United States concluded a deal on April 1, 2007 and signed it on June 30, 2007. After the signing of the agreement, however, the two countries struggled with even tougher legislative ratification processes. On 3 December 2010, additional negotiations were finally concluded. On October 12, 2011, the US Congress passed the agreement. About a month later after the congressional move, the National Assembly of South Korea also ratified the bilateral trade deal, thus finally ending a four-and-a-half-year legislative battle on both sides of the Pacific (Koo and Jho 2013: 66).

multi-track FTA strategy. The successful conclusion and/or ratification of FTA deals with major trading partners such as India, the EU and the United States during his presidency was not a coincidence (Koo 2013: 107–108).

From a regional comparative perspective, the speed and scope of South Korea's embrace of FTAs has been truly remarkable. The global economic crisis in 2008 has not slowed South Korea's drive to bilateral trade liberalization. If all of the fifteen FTAs that South Korea has concluded thus far were fully implemented, over 70% of its total trade would be governed by those agreements. South Korea's avid pursuit of bilateralism notwithstanding, the bottom line is that South Korea's new appetite for FTAs supplements its traditional endorsement of the WTO.

7.4.2   Major Players and Their Goals

South Korean trade policy remained passive and defensive as it was cocooned in the 'most-favored-nation' or MFN status in the GATT trading regime, while its market was shielded from international competition thanks to its 'developing country' status. Both trade agencies and their officials had little policy autonomy at the domestic level, as mercantilist ideas prevailed throughout the 1980s.

In the past, key players in South Korea's trade policy circle included the Blue House, the National Assembly, line ministries such as the Economic Planning Board (EPB), the Ministry of Finance (MOF), the Ministry of Foreign Affairs (MOFA), the Ministry of Agriculture and Fisheries (MAF), the Ministry of the Industry (MOI), and business interest groups such as the Federation of Korean Industries, the National Federation of Farmers Associations, and trade unions. Official negotiations with trading partners were headed by the MOFA, but the EPB played a more important role in coordinating the differences among different ministries and interest groups and in mandating the trade policy goals and strategies to the MOFA.

As its dependence on trade grew rapidly, however, South Korea's mercantilist trade policy came under heavy pressure to the point that it was no longer sustainable. At the domestic level, many were disappointed by the lack of strategy, competence, and leadership within the government during the UR negotiations. In particular, the lukewarm performance of trade negotiators during the rice negotiation prompted the need for a specialized government agency in charge of international negotiations. When President Kim Young-sam (1993–1998) came to office, he launched a government reorganization and created the Ministry of Trade and Industry (MOTI) in 1994.

Mandated for both trade liberalization and industrial protection, the MOTI soon faced a dilemma similar to the father with two daughters in Aesop's fable: one was married to a gardener wishing for rain and the other to a tile-maker wishing for dry weather. South Korea's international trade as a share of its GDP reached 56% in 1997. Securing preferential access to export markets in a more binding manner than provided by the WTO regime became an urgent concern, but the MOTI's policy direction was lost in such a dilemma.

The creation of the OMT in 1998 came at a critical juncture. The OMT was established under the Ministry of Foreign Affairs and Trade (MOFAT) to focus on trade liberalization negotiations, without worrying too much about protecting uncompetitive domestic industries. The MOFAT/OMT was also in charge of coordinating ministerial differences in policy options. In principal, other ministries would collaborate with the OMT by dispatching their personnel to trade negotiation delegations headed by the OMT. Institutionally embedded within the Ministry of Foreign Affairs and Trade, the OMT was insulated from the pressure of specific interest groups and was thus able to focus on broader national interests.[8]

The OMT demonstrated South Korea's renewed enthusiasm for and commitment to international trade. At the beginning, the OMT was beleaguered by other government agencies and interest groups favoring protectionism. But the new institution gradually established itself within the government with a mandate to initiate and negotiate bilateral trade deals. Its empowerment after 2004 institutionally reinforced chief negotiator autonomy *vis-à-vis* trade negotiations.[9] Combined with the free-trade ideas of chief negotiators as well as its own institutional interests, strengthened autonomy allowed the OMT to negotiate comprehensive trade deals without worrying too much about the protectionist elements within and outside the government (Koo and Jho 2013: 67–68).

The top-down nature of South Korea's FTA initiative as promoted by the OMT indicated that its FTA strategy was inherently developmentalist in tone and scope. The Roh government argued that an FTA with the United States would most likely benefit South Korean competitive sectors such as automobiles and textiles, while a variety of side-payments rather than blind protectionism would effectively mitigate the damage resulting from greater trade openness (Koo 2010: 108).

However, the downside of OMT policy autonomy and political insulation was that it was difficult for the trade agency to garner public support for trade deals, particularly during the ratification phase. Most notably, the OMT was criticized for its failure and incompetence in pacifying the protectionist outcry after the KORUS FTA was concluded. As a matter of fact, it was the former Ministry of Finance and Economy (currently the Ministry of Strategy and Finance) that was in

---

[8]However, inter-ministerial coordination was by no means easy within South Korean bureaucracy, especially when the counterpart had strong client groups. For instance, serious conflicts were reported between the OMT and the MAFF over the timing and scope of market opening for rice and beef products before, during and after the KORUS FTA negotiations. The MAFF argued that the right to regulate the safety of agricultural products and to promote food security belongs to the importing country. In rejection of sectoral protectionism, the OMT firmly took a pro-trade position that liberalizing agricultural sectors is necessary to improve competitiveness in the global market. The OMT, keeping a distance from the sectoral interests of industries and from client-based ministries, formulated and implemented independent negotiation agendas (Koo and Jho 2013: 79).

[9]With FTA negotiations orchestrated by the OMT under President Roh, liberal and legally-minded OMT officials were able to secure their preferences. The growing power of the OMT was emphasized by the appointment of its third Trade Minister, Kim Hyun-chong, in July 2004 as well as the promotion of its first Trade Minister, Han Duk-soo, to the post of Deputy Prime Minister and Minister of Finance and Economy (Koo 2009: 189).

charge of 'domestic' negotiations. Nevertheless, the OMT attracted all the public criticism due to its prominent status as a chief negotiator (Koo 2010: 114).

The OMT's impressive performance as a chief trade negotiator came with collateral damage in domestic politics, which would eventually be its undoing. Sectoral interests such as small and medium-sized firms and farmers threatened by greater liberalization cried for a trade policy reform, denouncing the broad national but abstract interests pursued by the OMT. More generally, there was a greater demand for democracy in trade negotiations as opposed to the top-down, elite-driven foreign negotiations and domestic communications.

Within government bureaucracy, the Ministry of Knowledge Economy (MKE), formerly the MOTI, capitalized on the growing demand for industrial promotion and waged a campaign to reclaim trade negotiating authority from the MOFAT/OMT. Upon taking office as the newly elected president, Park Geun-hye abolished the OMT and delegated negotiation authority to the newly established Ministry of Trade, Industry and Energy (MTIE) in 2013.

The Act on Governing Procedures of Conclusion and Implementation of Trade Treaties (also called the Trade Treaty Conclusion Procedure Act) was enacted on December 30, 2011 in the aftermath of the controversy over the Korea-US Free Trade Agreement, which was allegedly plagued by lack of transparency and accountability. This Act aimed to introduce a procedural framework for future negotiations as well as conclusion and implementation of trade agreements. It is designed to ensure greater transparency and accountability through the participation of the National Assembly and domestic interest groups during the various stages of trade negotiations ranging from whether to initiate treaty negotiations with trading partners to how to implement concluded treaties.

As summarized in Table 7.2, the governance structure of trade negotiations now consists of the National Assembly and three ministries: MOSF, MOFA, and MOTIE. The new governance system has seemingly improved coordination between international and domestic negotiations, while expanding the participation of traditionally under-represented groups and entities in the trade policymaking and negotiation process.

However, trade negotiation authority remains inherently fragmented among the three ministries, for instance, depending on whether it is a bilateral or multilateral negotiation and/or whether it relates to trade in goods or services. According to Hong (2014), government reorganization has changed organizational behavior to be more defensive against each other, while making trade officials more sensitive and vulnerable to protectionist interests. Meanwhile, the Trade Treaty Conclusion Procedure Act contains ambiguities in some of the key terms and the scope of its application. This potential confusion and complexity are likely to seriously delay the trade policymaking process (Lee 2012).

In sum, South Korea's current trade negotiation authority is in flux. More broadly, South Korea's trade policy now faces a different kind of dilemma: democracy versus trade liberalization. During the FTA negotiations in the 2000s, the South Korean government effectively pacified the domestic groups that would be negatively affected by trade liberalization by providing short-term side

Table 7.2 Governance of trade negotiations in the Park administration

	Ministry of Strategy and Finance	Ministry of Foreign Affairs	Ministry of Trade, Industry and Energy
Government Organization Act of 2013	– International economic and trade strategy and policy – Domestic negotiations and policy coordination relating FTAs and investment agreements with large economies and – Domestic negotiations and policy coordination relating the WTO Doha Development Agenda	– Economic diplomacy – International and regional economic cooperation (WTO, APEC, ASEM, ASEAN+3, etc.) – Bilateral economic cooperation with a focus on East Asia, Europe, and North America	– FTA negotiation – Trade policy relating the WTO, North America, Europe, East Asia, Middle East and Africa – East Asian free trade cooperation – Trade/industrial promotion
	National Assembly		
Trade Treaty Conclusion Procedure Act of 2011	– Procedural requirements for the government and the National Assembly from the decision of initiating treaty negotiations to concluding treaties to the implementation of concluded treaties – Ensuring broader discussions of key trade issues and wider participation of interest groups		

Source Collected and summarized by the author

payments. Such a strategy is no longer working as a growing number of South Korean citizens want their government to negotiate trade treaties in a more effective, democratic manner.

7.5   Conclusion and Policy Implications

This chapter examined how and the extent to which South Korea's trade policy has responded to internal challenges and external crises by repositioning, adapting, and restructuring its policy ideas and institutions. The political, social and economic conditions that underpinned South Korea's traditional trade policy paradigm came under scrutiny in the second half of the 1990s. The growing pressure for trade liberalization as a result of the UR and the outbreak of the Asian financial crisis in 1997–98 was a painful wake-up call for change.

South Korea remains committed to its obligations under the WTO. But the most prominent feature of its policy transformation is its embrace of comprehensive trade liberalization through preferential trading arrangements. In terms of issue scope and strength, South Korea has been one of the most active players in the proliferating web of regional and transregional FTAs. Such a policy shift is particularly intriguing because South Korea has not only been one of the principal beneficiaries of post-war multilateral trading regimes, but has also been criticized for its allegedly protectionist policies.

Institutionally, this change from developmental mercantilism to developmental liberalism was made possible by the OMT. Even with greater trade liberalization, the South Korean government opted to maintain the legacies of the developmental state, with the government still playing an important role in planning, implementing, and sustaining trade reforms.

Equally important, however, is the growing need for transparency in and accountability for trade liberalization, which has set the new political dynamics of policymaking and policy implementation. The sudden demise of the OMT in 2013 shows that the governance of trade policymaking and negotiations is in flux, if not in complete disarray.

South Korea's trade policy now faces a new dilemma between democracy and trade openness. During rapid trade liberalization through FTAs in the 2000s, the South Korean government effectively pacified domestic constituents who would be negatively affected by providing short-term but generous compensations. Such a developmental-liberal strategy is no longer working as a growing proportion of the South Korean public wants their government to negotiate trade treaties in a more effective, democratic manner.

It is unclear whether such a dual demand for greater democracy and greater trade openness will transform South Korea's trade policy once again from top-down, developmental liberalism to bottom-up, market-based liberalism. This is a question that warrants further study, as the ongoing adjustment and adaptation of South Korea's trade policy defies any clear demarcation between developmentalism and liberalism.

In conclusion, democracy may have a negative impact on trade openness in the short-run, possibly due to the exacerbation of distributional conflicts. However, as the South Korean case has shown and will continue to show, democracy is likely to induce more trade openness in the long-run as democracy makes it harder for governments to use trade barriers as a means of increasing political support.

References

Aggarwal VK, Koo MG (2008) Asia's new institutional architecture: evolving structures for managing trade, financial, and security relations. Springer, New York

Aggarwal VK, Koo MG (2016) Designing trade institutions for Asia. In: Pekkanen SM (ed) Asian designs: interests, identities, and states in external institutions. Oxford University Press, London, pp 35–58

Aggarwal VK, Lee S (2011) The domestic political economy of preferential trade agreements. In: Aggarwal VK, Lee S (eds) Trade policy in The Asia-Pacific: the role of ideas, interests, and institutions. Springer, New York, pp 1–28

Aggarwal VK, Urata S (2006) Bilateral trade agreements in the Asia-Pacific: origins, evolution, and implications. Routledge, New York

Dent C (2006) New free trade agreements in the Asia Pacific: towards lattice regionalism?. Palgrave Macmillan, New York

Dieter H (2009) Changing patterns of regional governance: from security to political economy? Pac Rev 22(1):73–90

Encarnation DJ (ed) (1999) Japanese multinationals in Asia: regional operations in comparative perspective. Oxford University Press, New York

Hong S (2014) The changes and continuities of Korean government's international trade policy: an analysis on the reshuffle of trade administrative system of park administration. Korea Trade Rev 39(3):261–292 (in Korean)

International Monetary Fund (2014) Regional economic outlook: Asia and Pacific sustaining the momentum: vigilance and reforms. International Monetary Fund, Washington, D.C.

Katzenstein PJ (2005) A world of regions: Asia and Europe in the American imperium. Cornell University Press, Ithaca

Kennedy D, Nicholas A (2009) The impact of perceived export barriers on export performance: a case study of Ghanaian non-traditional firms. Master's thesis, The Bodø Graduate School of Business

Koo MG (2006) From multilateralism to bilateralism? A shift in South Korea's trade strategy. In: Aggarwal VK, Urata S (eds) Bilateral trade agreements in the Asia-Pacific: origins, evolution, and implications. Routledge, New York

Koo MG (2009) South Korea's FTAs: moving from an emulative to a competitive strategy. In: Solís M, Stallings B, Katada SN (eds) Competitive regionalism: FTA diffusion in the Pacific Rim. Palgrave, New York

Koo MG (2010) Embracing free trade agreements, Korean Style: from developmental mercantilism to developmental liberalism. Korean J Policy Stud 25(3):101–123

Koo MG (2013) Trade policy for development: paradigm shift from mercantilism to liberalism. In: Kwon H, Koo MG (eds) The Korean government and public policies in a development nexus, vol 1. Springer, New York, pp 95–113

Koo MG, Jho W (2013) Linking domestic decision-making and international bargaining results: beef and automobile negotiations between South Korea and the United States. Int Relat Asia Pac 13(1):65–93

Lee JM (2012) South Korea's Trade Treaty Conclusion Procedure Act and its prospects. Seoul Int Law J 19(1):31–62 (in Korean)

Lee S (2006) The political economy of the Korea-U.S. FTA: The Korean government's FTA strategy revisited. Paper Presented at the Convention of the Association of Korean Political and Diplomatic History (in Korean)

Lee S, Han T (2006) The demise of 'Korea, Inc'.: Paradigm shift in Korea's developmental state. J Contemp Asia 36(3):305–324

Lee S, Moon C (2008) South Korea's regional economic cooperation policy: the evolution of an adaptive strategy. In: Aggarwal VK, Koo MG, Lee S, Moon C (eds) Northeast Asian regionalism: ripe for integration?. Springer, New York, pp 37–61

Lester S, Mercurio B, Davies A (2012) World trade law: text, materials and commentary. Hart Publishing, Oxford and Portland

Mo J, Moon C (1999) Korea after the crash. J Democracy 10(3):150–164

Moon C, Yoon D (2011) Industrial policy in an integrated world economy: the South Korean paradox. In: Claes DH, Knutsen CH (eds) Governing the global economy: politics, institutions and economic development. Routledge, London and New York

Pempel TJ (2010) Soft balancing, hedging, and institutional darwinism: the economic-security nexus and East Asian regionalism. J East Asian Stud 10(2):209–238

Ravenhill J (2001) APEC and the construction of Asia-Pacific regionalism. Cambridge University Press, Cambridge

Sohn Y (2006) The political economy of FTA in Korea: an IPE perspective. J World Politics 27(2):93–133

Sohn Y, Koo MG (2011) Securitizing trade: the case of the Korea-U.S. free trade agreement. Int Relat Asia Pac 11(3):433–460

Solís M, Stallings B, Katada SN (eds) (2009) Competitive regionalism: FTA diffusion in the Pacific Rim. Palgrave Macmillan, New York

World Trade Organization (2012) Trade policy review: Republic of Korea. https://www.wto.org/english/tratop_e/tpr_e/tp368e.htm

Chapter 8
The Challenges of Foreign Policy and Suggestions for Future Responses

Byoung Kwon Sohn

8.1 Introduction

The Korean Peninsula was one of the powder kegs of the East-West confrontation during the Cold War. Beginning with the end of the Second World War, the northern and southern parts of the Korea Peninsula were separately occupied by the Soviet Union and the US, respectively, along the 38th parallel, and the division was made virtually permanent after the end of the Korean War without a clear winner. Korea has since remained a solid security ally of the US, while North Korea has been under the military and economic protection of first the Soviet Union and then China.

After the end of the Cold War in the last days of the 1980s, Korea began to normalize its diplomatic relations with Russia, China, and former socialist countries in Eastern Europe with great success. Led by President Roh Tae-woo, the so-called "Northern Diplomacy" (Nordpolitik) gave Korea a huge space for diplomatic maneuvering. In contrast, North Korea embarked on a path toward a nuclear-armed nation to break out of diplomatic deadlock. As a matter of fact, trade between China and Korea began to increase at an accelerating speed in the 1990s and 2000s, thus scaling up the relationship of the two nations, while North Korea fell into economic misery due to productivity decline and international sanctions.

Amid the constant tension on the Korean Peninsula, the US-China relationship has begun to sour since the Obama administration announced its proactive posture toward Asia (Obama 2009; Clinton 2010, 2011). As China sees the US position of "pivoting" or "rebalancing" as a disguised name for encircling China, Korea also has to pay more attention to the increasingly conflict-prone relationship between the US and China in the region. Despite US assurances that it welcomes a peaceful and prosperous China and that the US's focus on Asia is due to its strategic and economic importance, China suspects the US of intending to contain China with the

B.K. Sohn (✉)
Chung-Ang University, Seoul, South Korea
e-mail: byoungk@chol.com

© Springer International Publishing AG 2017
J. Choi et al. (eds.), *The Korean Government and Public Policies in a Development Nexus*, The Political Economy of the Asia Pacific,
DOI 10.1007/978-3-319-52473-3_8

help of Japan. This new development is quite worrisome to Korea, which has been a traditional security ally of the US, and which at the same time has become dependent on China in a trade relationship.

On the other hand, Korean democratization in 1987 and the domestic political evolution thereafter made the Korean foreign policy-making process more complicated at best. Such domestic constituencies as interest and citizen groups, the media, public opinion, and the National Assembly all became meaningful elements the Korean government has to take into account in formulating foreign policy. Partisan politics also infiltrated foreign policy issues, making it more difficult to achieve bipartisan policy initiatives.

Against this background of the tense security situation in Northeast Asia and the increasing importance of the domestic dimension in Korean foreign policy-making, this article attempts to articulate a list of Korean foreign policy challenges, and to propose in turn a set of suggestions for future response. For this purpose, the article identifies the following items as the gravest challenges for Korea to address: domestic demands from democratized Korea, Korea's security posture in transition, the North Korean conundrum, and the need to invest more in public and middle power diplomacy. After articulating these challenges, this article also suggests a set of future policy responses. Finally, in the conclusion the whole argument will be summarized in a condensed fashion.[1]

8.2   Challenges for Korean Foreign Policy

8.2.1   Demands from Democratized Domestic Politics

During the authoritarian rule in the 1970s through 1987, Korean foreign policy-making had been the exclusive realm of the president and his innermost personnel. In the midst of the Cold War on a global scale, the Korean president had been virtually the only person to dictate the terms and directions of foreign and security policy-making. No other government officials, including National Assembly members, and not to mention the media and the public, dared to challenge presidential authority in this policy area. Due to the lack of information and expertise and amid the monolithically strong anti-communist sentiment across the nation, public opinion and the National Assembly were not able to play any meaningful role (Lee 1993).

---

[1]For an overview of the history, players, and standard decision-making process of Korean foreign policy, see Lee and Kim (1993), Ministry of Foreign Affairs and Trade (2009), and Hamm and Namgung (2010). On the future tasks of Korean foreign policy in the early 21st century, see Ha (2013). On the Korean strategy in the context of the US-China rivalry in Asia, see Chun (2015).

This type of insulated, absolute, and top-down foreign policy-making process can no longer be sustained after the 1987 democratization. Although the foreign policy-making process is largely led by the government, it is hardly the only player in the game. The increasing demand from the public to know, the media's incessant search for information on governmental policy, and the enhanced status and power of the National Assembly brought about tremendous change in the landscape of the foreign policy-making process, rendering it inevitable for the president and his top staff to take domestic elements into account. A more detailed explanation will be provided as follows.

First of all, the 1987 democratization brought a variety of constituencies into the Korean foreign policy-making process. Domestic constituents were no longer docile followers of presidential guidelines, but they rather became stakeholders concerned about how the decisions made by the government would affect their lives. For example, Korean farmers have been the most vociferous players that Korean decision makers have to take into account when it comes to international trade agreement with foreign nations, such as the Korea-US FTA (Yu 2002; Lee 2003). Other citizen groups such as human rights advocacy organizations and environmental groups have also been involved in the foreign policy-making process of the government in one way or another.

On the other hand, party politics has also played its role in the post-democratization Korean foreign policy-making process, particularly with respect to inter-Korean matters and trade deals with foreign countries (Namgung 2004; Jaung 2008). More often than not, the foreign policy postures of the progressive and conservative parties have been so divergent that foreign policy almost became the realm of partisan politics.

There is no doubt that public opinion and the media also came to play a part in the Korean foreign policy-making process. Although not a major actor dictating the terms of foreign policy, public opinion sets the "national mood" which the government should not transgress in carrying out foreign policy. Given the strong national anti-Japanese sentiment, for example, the president finds it extremely difficult to make conciliatory gestures toward Japan, even when the latter shows some sign of remorse toward the Korean public. On the other hand, with SNS tools now widely available among the Korean public, the media, whether pro- or anti-government in its policy stance, can shape public opinion by framing the issues. Politicized in one sense or another, the media sometimes controls how the public interprets and evaluates political issues and events through its framing power.

In summary, domestic interest and advocacy groups, the National Assembly and political parties, public opinion and the media all influence the foreign policy-making process more strongly than during the authoritarian past. Although foreign policy-making is still initiated and led by the government as before, it is also true that non-governmental and legislative actors are getting more actively involved as well. In this changed environment, the Korean government is finding it harder to defend its policy initiatives against potential opposition.

8.2.2   Korea's Security Posture in Transition

Korea-US Alliance Facing New Demands

If nothing else, the solid Korea-US alliance has been the cornerstone not only for military deterrence against North Korea but also for Korean economic prosperity since the end of the Korean War. The US forces stationed in Korea have been the symbol of the US security commitment to Korea, and effectively prevented North Korea from making another full-scale invasion against South Korea. It would be little exaggeration to say that "the Korean developmental state" was nurtured under US security protection. The alliance, however, now faces new challenges coming from several directions.

Among other things, the traditional security-centered Korea-US alliance has recently been challenged to upgrade to the level of global partnership. In other words, the alliance should no longer be confined to the prevention of military hostilities on the Korean Peninsula, but is also asked to transform into a basis for the two nations' global cooperation in such areas as nuclear nonproliferation, climate change, and anti-terrorism. This new challenge calls on Korea to become a more active stakeholder in global affairs, carrying a share of the enlarged burden as a full US ally.

Secondly, the US strategy of rebalancing in Asia poses a grave dilemma for Korea, as it comes with a new set of US demands. Related to this, Korea has been continually urged by the US to assist when the US finds itself in discord with China. For example, the US requested Korea to stand on its side in the territorial disputes of the East and South China Seas (Korea Herald 2015).[2] There has been recent US pressure on Korea to come back into the dialogue with Japan amid the Korea-Japan discord over compensation for the comfort girl issue. This is in fact motivated by the ultimate US wish to maintain a close trilateral cooperation among Korea, Japan, and itself against Chinese assertiveness as well as against North Korean military provocation. As China interprets the US rebalancing as a disguised tactic for

---

[2]On the South China Sea issue, Korea was put into a dilemma when US President Obama asked President Park Geun-hye to speak publicly against China on the maritime territorial disputes in the South China Sea when she visited Washington in September 2015. To show Korean support, President Park said the issue should be resolved according to "the international agreement and code of conduct" during the East Asia Summit held in Kuala Lumpur, Malaysia in November 2015. That remark reflects a position similar to that she was reported to take during her visit to the US (JoongAng Daily 2015).

containing it, Korea finds it difficult to take an effective and prompt position when divisive issues arise between the US and China.

Finally, Korea's participation in the China-led AIIB (Asia Infrastructure Investment Bank) and RCEP (Regional Comprehensive Economic Partnership) negotiations while rejecting the previous US request for Korea to join TPP (Trans-Pacific Partnership) preparatory negotiations could make the US suspect that Korea is leaning toward China. Furthermore, Korea's ambiguous attitude on the THAAD (Terminal High Area Altitude Defense) system may have also made the US uneasy, and it still remains a thorny issue between the two allies.[3]

Were it not for the US rebalancing and the assertive rise of China, there would be little dilemma for Korea. As the Sino-American relationship becomes difficult, however, the Korean government is restricted in its policy choices. Given that, the gravest challenge for Korea is to maintain a solid Korea-US security partnership and not to give the US the misguided impression that Korea is now bandwagoning toward China.[4]

China's Influence Looming over East Asia

In addition to the complicated development facing the Korea-US alliance, another challenge of grave concern for Korea is the increasing influence of China in East Asia and its assertive foreign policy posture. As a matter of fact, China's increasingly proactive foreign policy posture concerns its security-sensitive neighbors, Korea being one of them. In fact, it has been quite a long time since China came into actual diplomatic conflict with the Philippines and Vietnam in the South China Sea, as well as with Japan in the East China Sea. On the other hand, as China sees the US strategy of rebalancing as a disguised attempt to encircle it and infringe on its "core interests", China has begun to accelerate military modernization, launching battleships further and further off its coast.

As China flexes its muscles on territorial issues, the US-China rivalry is intensifying in East Asia. The territorial disputes in the South and East China Seas will not be easily settled given the Chinese claim of "core interests" and "territorial sovereignty" and the US avowal of "right of free maritime navigation" in response.

---

[3]After the launch of the long-range missile by North Korea in February in 2016, however, Korea and the US finally signed the terms of reference on the composition of the Korea-US joint task force to discuss the THAAD installment in Korea.

[4]When Korea took pains to make President Park's visit to China understood to the US during her Washington visit in October in 2015, this type of dilemma was succinctly shown. According to the media report, the US was infuriated at President Park's participation in the military parade in Beijing, China, on the anniversary of Chinese victory in the Second World War. The US may have felt betrayed, although it cannot explicitly expose this genuine feeling in public. From the US perspective, the visit may have been untimely amid the US-China tension surrounding territorial issues. The alliance breach caused by the visit only appeared to be amended after President Park's Washington visit.

On the other hand, the final signing of the TPP, a US-led mega free trade agreement among the 12 nations around the Pacific Ocean, may also accelerate China's step toward creating its own free trade zone such as the RCEP (Regional Comprehensive Economic Partnership). This could make the two free trade regimes confront each other in the form of rivalry between exclusive economic blocs. Additionally, Japan's now assertive posture toward China has the possibility of making China even more aggressive toward Japan, and may drag the US to Japan's side in a potential conflict with China.

Under these circumstances, Korea has to first define what kind of relationship it should maintain with China given the supreme importance of the Korea-US alliance, which is more than 60 decades old. How can Korea accommodate its relationship with China, which still highly values the strategic, military, and geographic importance of North Korea, given its traditional security relationship with the US, which is at serious discord with China on some territorial issues? Since this conundrum cannot be dealt with through a zero-sum calculation, it poses a grave foreign policy challenge for top Korean decision-makers now and in the future. The bottom line, however, should be that Korea has to be careful not to give China such a mistaken image of Korea aligning against it with the US and Japan.

In addition to that, Korea has the difficult task of making sure China plays a more active role in North Korean issues. Despite China's reluctance to accept, one sure agreement is the preeminence of sanctioning power for China on North Korea when the latter provokes the global community by testing nuclear weapons and launching missiles. Given that, Korea needs to persuade China to realize that North Korea cannot remain a nation of permanent strategic value, and could someday become a strategic burden restricting China's future diplomatic discretion. In line with this, Korea has to think of ways to induce China to put effective sanctions on North Korea to make the latter truly accountable for its unwelcome activities.

Japan's Energized Assertiveness

It is widely recognized that Japan's overall security role in Northeast Asia has increased during the reign of Prime Minister Abe, and that it was made possible mostly by strong US support among other factors. Riding on the US strategy of Asia rebalancing and threatened by the increasing assertiveness of China as well as the risk-taking ventures of Kim Jung-un's North Korea, Japan decided to become a "normal state" with "collective self-defense" capability.

Neither the enhanced security role of Japan nor Abe's strong conservative turn, however, is welcomed by the Korean government and the Korean public. The reason is self-evident in that Korea still lives with a vivid memory of the brutal Japanese imperial rule during the early half of the 20th century. As a matter of fact, the Japanese government's overall reluctance to publicly apologize for its inhumane treatment of colonial people only infuriates Korean citizens. The comfort girl issue, in particular, deeply angers the Korean people despite the recent Japanese public apology, and still remains a wedge issue between the two nations.[5] To make matters worse, the incessant self-justifying remarks by Japanese politicians regarding colonial rule of Korea and Tokdo Island (Takeshima Island in Japanese) has only became fodder for continuing anti-Japanese sentiment in Korea.

Despite that, there is widespread consensus among Korean foreign policy experts that Korea should seek a way out of this deadlocked situation with Japan. The US, Korea's closest security partner, is also pressuring Korea to get back on a normal track with Japan at a time when China looms larger in the region and when North Korea is becoming more provocative. In its turn, Korea also feels the need to consult with Japan on North Korean matters, and to restore the economic, social, and cultural exchanges to the previous level. What kind of steps to take and what sort of issues to discuss with Japan, as well as to what extent cooperation should be achieved are all difficult questions to be addressed.

At the same time, Korea should be careful in resuming policy coordination lest this should be suspected as a measure for resuscitating the trilateral security cooperation among Korea, the US, and Japan aimed at China. In other words, Korea needs to figure out the extent to which and the conditions under which it should pursue a cooperative relationship with Japan given the increasing influence of China on issues related to the Korean Peninsula. Should Korea damage its common front with Japan on the North Korean nuclear issue simply by blaming Japan together with China for its atrocities during the Second World War? What other factors should Korea take into account for more effective cooperation with Japan, other than simply protesting against Japan's repeated provocative behavior? These delicate but important issues should be meticulously discussed and addressed accordingly.

8.2.3 North Korean Security Threat

Since the end of the Korean War, North Korea has been the main source of Korean national security threat. Despite the visits of Presidents Kim Dae-jung and Roh Moo-hyun to Pyongyang for inter-Korean reconciliation in 2000 and 2007 respectively, North Korea has never stopped provoking Korea from time to time. North Korea conducted its first nuclear test in 2006 and completed its fourth test on January 6, 2016, despite a series of UN sanctions already put into effect against it. North Korea even infiltrated Korea to secretly blow up a Korean patrol battleship, the Chonanham, on March 26, 2010 and later bombarded Yonyoung Island, the home of many Korean fishermen, on November 23 in the same year.

---

[5]Japanese Foreign Minister Fumio Kishida, on behalf of Prime Minister Abe, publicly apologized to Korea on the comfort girl issue on December 28, 2015 after he agreed with Korean Foreign Minister Yoon on the final deal on the governmental level. Many Korean citizens are not satisfied with the apology, especially because Prime Minister Abe refused to directly apologize to the victims who suffered as comfort girl for the Japanese imperial army during the Second World War.

Korea, for its part, had no choice but to retaliate in various ways. After the Chonanham incident in 2010, the conservative Lee Myung-bak Administration initiated the so-called "May 24 Measures" which halted inter-Korean trade, humanitarian assistance, and new investment, leaving only the Kaesong Industrial Complex intact. The Kaesong Industrial Complex, a legacy of President Kim Dae-jung's Sunshine Policy toward North Korea, was also eventually closed by the Park Geun-hye Administration, another conservative government, after the fourth North Korean nuclear test on January 6 and the consequent long-range missile launch on February 7, 2016.

Along with these measures of Korean retaliation, the international community also cooperated individually and collectively. The UN Security Council has denounced North Korean nuclear and missile tests over the last decade or so. Most recently after the fourth North Korean nuclear test and the consequent missile launch, it also passed Resolution 2270 on March 2, 2016, the strongest resolution ever sanctioning North Korea. Pushed by Korea and the US, China also promised to fully cooperate with the UN Security Council. The US also passed its own individual resolution sanctioning North Korea in Congress on February 12, days before the UN sanction. Korea followed suit by announcing its own measures sanctioning North Korea with respect to financial transactions and maritime affairs on March 8.

Now the dilemma for Korea is that North Korea has shown little sign of relenting its provocation and nuclear efforts, despite Korean retaliatory measures and international sanctions. Contending that the nuclear armament is a choice for self-defense against US hostilities, North Korea seems to be envisioning itself as a nuclear-armed great power. Facing North Korea's stubborn position, Korea has to think of a way to prevent North Korea from continuing such risky provocation. At the same time, Korea has to figure out a plan to bring North Korea back to the dialogue table. The Korean government cannot let the Kaesong Industrial Complex remain permanently closed, and cannot keep the inter-Korean relationship endlessly suspended.

On the other hand, Korea also has to design a path for an endurable peace regime on the Korean Peninsula, including a sustainable reunification blueprint. In its turn, Korea's reunification policy also has to deal with North Korea's doctrine that military and political questions should be addressed first ahead of any other matters. That stance is in sharp contrast to the conventional Korean position that the reunification process should start with exchanges of a non-military and non-political nature. To make matters even more complicated, the military part of the reunification process inevitably has to address the dismantling of the North Korean nuclear program, and also has to discuss how to create conditions for permanent peace on the Korean Peninsula in place of the current armistice.

In short, Korea should figure out the best way to dismantle and freeze North Korean nuclear progress and at the same time to resume a productive inter-Korea dialogue along with the 6-party talk. In the past, North Korea has made some short-term gestures to show that it tries its best to mitigate tension, but these are generally revoked sooner or later, only deepening distrust toward North Korea. Without mutual trust amid the repeated making and breaking of commitments, the vicious cycle will only continue. Korea now needs to create a virtuous circle anew.

8.2.4 Public and Middle Power Diplomacy in Great Demand[6]

After the end of the Cold War, the importance of soft power and public diplomacy has been emphasized in the foreign policy-making process across nations. Defined as the power to make other nations attracted to a certain nation, soft power has become a very important foreign policy tool along with hard power (Nye 2004).[7] As foreign policy-makers began to believe that resorting to military means is too costly to sustain, the notion of soft power gained traction among foreign policy communities across the globe, particularly after the end of the Cold War.

As a corollary, public diplomacy has also become crucial, particularly in this globalized information society. Aiming at the public of a target nation, public diplomacy attempts to implant benign images of the sender nation in the public of the target nation by building multiple non-governmental channels to export culture, to provide development and humanitarian assistance, and to exchange students and scholars among nations (Cull 2008). As the global society becomes connected by SNS networks, the art of persuading the public of the target nation has become an integral element of the foreign policy-making process of the sender state.

As one of the member states of the OECD and as a model nation having achieved both democratization and economic development, Korea is regarded as one of the few nations which is well positioned to pursue a middle power strategy by resorting to soft power and public diplomacy (Chun and Choo 2013: 104–105). Compared with the US, China, and Japan, Korea is in an advantaged position to work as a friendlier diplomatic partner with developing nations in that Korea is a middle-sized nation without any history of militarized rivalry of its own initiation. In contrast to the neighboring great powers with intense rivalry among themselves and a larger size and scale in terms of GDP, population, and territory, Korea is much better positioned to attract developing nations, and thus can play the role of messenger between them and more advanced nations.

In a similar vein, many policy-makers and intellectuals in the international community as well as inside Korea recommend that Korea contribute its due part corresponding to Korea's enhanced global status. This, however, should come as a challenge to Korea, which is now suffering from tight budget constraints caused by the increase in welfare and infrastructure spending plus constant defense spending.

---

[6]On the notion of public diplomacy and its sub-categories, see Cull (2008). On the public diplomacy strategies in the East Asian international relations and of Korea, see Melissen and Sohn (2015). On the notion of middle power diplomacy, see Cooper (1997) and Kim (2009). See Lee (2012) for the Korean middle power strategy in particular.

[7]While hard power, such as economic and military resources, is utilized to achieve immediate foreign policy goals, soft power is conceived of as a "milieu power", a kind of power providing a context within which a nation can create favorable diplomatic conditions on a longer-term level. For more specifics on the notion of hard and soft power, see Chap. 1 of Nye (2004).

Therefore, how to pursue a more effective middle power diplomacy, and thus how to upgrade its global image through public diplomacy are great challenges facing Korea.

8.3   Suggestions for Korean Foreign Policy

8.3.1   Pursuing Principled Foreign Policy

The first and foremost task for Korean foreign policy should be to determine what principles Korea should pursue when it actually conducts policies on a daily basis. Once these principles are selected, Korea should be consistent in evoking and applying them to make its commitment to these principles credible. Setting up basic foreign policy principles first and then consistently applying them is increasingly important in that Korean foreign policy options should look well-coordinated to the eyes of the international community.[8]

What kind of priorities, ideas, or policy directions could count among the principles that should guide the overall contours of Korean foreign policy? In the most general sense, they could include the ideas, priorities, and general policy directions which have guided Korean foreign policy with widespread domestic consensus, and which have also been emphasized throughout the administrations, although with some variation.

For example, the guiding principles could entail permanent maintenance of Korean sovereignty and territorial integrity, peaceful inter-Korean reunification, Korean economic prosperity, international cooperation for peace, prosperity and human rights, and respect for international law and institutions. These are selected by the author somewhat arbitrarily, but these principles are not entirely new ones. They are believed to have been mentioned and drawn upon in the foreign policy community as general guidelines for the effective conduct of Korean foreign policy.

8.3.2   Seeking Domestic Consensus for Effective Foreign Policy

There is no doubt that effective foreign policy implementation needs domestic support in a liberal democracy. Korea has been no exception, particularly after the democratization in 1987. In this sense, it will help a great deal for common ground

---

[8]Putting forward the so-called "national interest' for justifying specific policy options as a situation develops does not deliver much. It is because the "national interest" may appear as an ad hoc rationale for circumstance-driven policy options when they are not backed by a consistent set of principles. In one sense or another, the actions of whichever sort, once taken by the authority of the government, could be justified as an action for national interest whether they truly are so or not.

to be forged through sustained dialogue among government elites, foreign policy experts, and the general public. The Korean foreign policy decision-makers, including the president, should therefore consider public sentiment as an important input element in figuring out what could constitute common ground with the public.

Given the need to take into account public sentiment, the foreign policy-makers should utilize multiple channels in communicating with the public. There are options for various modes with respect to the extent to which foreign policy-related information can be shared with the public depending on specific issues. The first mode is to share with the public what the government knows in the policy-making process as far as sharing does not interfere with national security. If the public is persuaded by the government's public relations efforts, it will reinforce the government's position and strengthen its bargaining position vis-a-vis the foreign counterparts at the negotiating table.

If the public opposes the government's position, the latter has to reconsider its policy stance and may have to change it. If the government really believes that Korea needs to pursue the policy, however, it will have to make every effort to overcome public opposition by highlighting the urgency of the policy. On the other hand, if there is no opposition from the start, the government can initiate policy with a solid base of domestic consensus. In whichever case, the public may appreciate the government's endeavor to obtain feedback from the public on foreign policy matters, and if the effort is successfully exercised, the dialogue with the public will have the effect of strengthening the legitimacy of the policy.

The second mode of communicating with the public is to simply follow the traditional secret diplomacy when it is judged inevitable by the government to do so. While some foreign policy related-information can be revealed to and shared with the public, other highly classified or national security-related information should be shared only among the innermost top decision-makers. Otherwise, the Korean government's policy options could be restricted from the start as well as at the negotiating table as a result of information leaks. Depending on the issues at stake, the government should be flexible in choosing the mode of sharing information with the public.

One final point to note is that the government also has to utilize SNS and other advanced communication technology to advocate its foreign policy position to the public. For this public relations purpose, the government should more actively resort to the use of web and social media (e-mails, Facebook) as a way to get messages across to the public. While the utilization of the traditional means of communication such as government-financed public broadcasting can give the impression of one-sided government propagandizing, the more public-friendly strategy of resorting to SNS media can be more effective for citizens inclined to use to social media in everyday life, particularly young people.

8.3.3   Searching for a Sustainable Diplomatic Path in Northeast Asia

Preparing the Korea-US Relationship for the 21st Century
Given the enhanced Korean standing on the global scene and the need to upgrade the Korea-US alliance, Korea should play a more active role as a global partner of the US while constantly confirming the tight solidarity of the military cooperation between the two nations on matters related to the security of Korea. As a member state of the OECD and as a global partner of the US, Korea should broaden its perspective beyond the Korean Peninsula and Northeast Asia, and invest more in global affairs such as development aid, climate change, anti-terrorism, and UN peace-keeping operations. When Korea accumulates this type of "global social capital" along with the US, Korea will be entitled to ask the US to play its due part in matters related to Korean security in return for these contributions.

Additionally, Korea should share the military burden when asked by the US, but should refuse inordinate requests from the US. With the huge budget deficit accumulated amid the financial crisis since 2007, the US has asked its Northeast allies such as Korea and Japan to share more of the defense burden. While not refusing to pay its due share, Korea should also be ready to bring up its own difficult domestic economic situation as an excuse when requests from the US are deemed unacceptable. In line with that, a strategic linking of Korea's due share with its own wish list for US reciprocal cooperation in other defense policy areas could be considered.

Given the vital importance of the security cooperation between Korea and the US and amid the increasingly tense relationship between the US and China regarding the US's Asia rebalancing stance, Korea should be on alert to prevent the two giants from coming into conflict on matters related to the Korean Peninsula and Northeast Asia. The tense relationship between the two giants only restricts Korea's diplomatic discretion, forcing Korea to choose sides, which would be the worst scenario imaginable. As a nation located between China and the US, Korea should prevent this scenario from being played out, and needs to play a messenger role for the two nations not to come into conflict due to mutual misunderstanding.

Related to the conflict potential between the US and China, one of the most important tasks for Korea is to make sure that the US does not misconstrue its outreach toward China. Korea needs to explain to the US that the Korea-US military alliance will not be affected by the deepening of the Korea-China cooperation, and to emphasize that the Korea-China relationship is embedded in security solidarity between Korea and the US. In a nutshell, Korea should take care not to give false impressions to the US, for example, that Korea is drawing closer to China in an attempt to gain leverage in its interactions with the US.

Accommodating China's Rise
As previously discussed, Korea needs to carefully manage the Sino-American relationship lest the relationship of the two nations regarding the Korean Peninsula

deteriorates. The intensification of the rivalry will only restrict Korean diplomatic space in dealing with North Korea, and could make the Korea-US alliance rather lean toward containing China. Despite these concerns, the rise of China and the US's Asia rebalancing have inevitably made the US-China relationship tense.

Under these complicated circumstances, Korea needs to develop multiple channels of dialogue with China across a broad range of issues. Just as Korea resolves policy discordance with the US through multiple channels long established across ministerial levels, Korea needs to explore as many communication channels as possible with China to prevent mutual misperception from damaging their relationship. This may help Korea to deliver genuine intentions more effectively and in a more straightforward fashion to China, which could come to suspect that Korea is only working as a faithful ally of the US.

In line with this, Korea needs to broaden its participation in China-led project initiatives if it fits Korean foreign policy principles and does not damage its national interests. The Korean decision to join the AIIB and to participate in the RCEP preparatory negotiations should be appreciated in that respect. Furthermore, Korea should continue to find ways for mutual cooperation with China which will contribute to trust-building in the long-term perspective. Cultural and educational exchange, promotion of the Korean Stream in China (the public's attraction to Korean pop culture), and the accommodation of more Chinese tourists will help in this endeavor.

Turning to the security issues surrounding the Korean Peninsula, Korea needs to assure China that the Korea-US alliance does not aim to contain China, at least not for the Korean part. For this purpose, Korea should attempt to build and institutionalize a kind of trilateral dialogue among Korea, the US, and China to address the North Korean nuclear issue and other security issues concerning Northeast Asia. It could be implemented within or alongside the 6-party talk, or be attempted independently outside this framework.

Addressing Assertive Japan

Korean foreign policy toward Japan should proceed on two separate tracks: one for security, economic and cultural cooperation for the future, and another for resolving the traditional acrimony between the two nations. Korean should make sure, however, that sluggish procession in one track should not overly affect the progress on the other track lest the interaction of the two nations face a total gridlock across the whole range of issues.

In fact, Japan is one of the strategically most important nations and a historically close neighbor to Korea. Given this geographic and historical destiny, Korea should keep talking with Japan through various channels so that the diplomacy between the two nations works on a continuing basis. For this purpose, the Korean foreign policy-makers should not always dance to the rhythm of public sentiment. They should rather be able to persuade Korean citizens not to see the Korea-Japan relationship only from the perspective of the painful colonial past.

In addition to the need for cooperation and reconciliation, Korea should keep a watchful eye on the enhanced security role of Japan. As Japan is geared up for a more active defense role in Northeast Asia as a US security partner and as a spearhead nation of the US's Asia rebalancing, Korean should be on alert against potential negative impacts, and make meticulous contingency plans accordingly. In particular, as Japan takes the collective self-defense role in the region, Korea has to evaluate what it could mean in the worst-case emergencies surrounding the Korean Peninsula, and should make appropriate preparations in advance.

Finally, amid the rampant and rising anti-Korean sentiment in Japan, Korea should pay more attention to Japanese public sentiment and invest more in public diplomacy toward the Japanese to mitigate these negative feelings. As matter of fact, the confrontation between the two nations was initially formed by political leaders, not by citizens. To reverse the negative anti-Korean mood in Japan, the Korean government should restart exchange programs at the civilian level first, including tourism, educational and cultural interactions, as well as trade and financial cooperation so that the two nations can repair their scarred relationship.

8.3.4   Dealing with North Korean Provocation

The first and foremost task for Korea in inter-Korean matters would be preventing North Korea from further provocation with nuclear and missile tests, as well as getting North Korea back to the dialogue table, helping it to be open to the international community, and eventually reunifying. To achieve this goal, Korea should be flexible enough to respond to North Korea by using both sanctions and positive rewards as situations develop, in close cooperation with the US, China, and the international community. The bottom line is that Korea has to figure out the best ways of changing North Korean behavior to its benefit.

More specifically, when North Korea continues to risk provocation with nuclear and missile tests despite the warnings of the international community, Korea should be aware that the best way to stop it may be substantial negative sanctions in close cooperation with the UN and other major stakeholder nations. As matter of fact, the UN Security Council, backed by both the US and China, has passed several resolutions sanctioning North Korea. In light of these sanctions on North Korea, Korea should be able to urge China, the host nation of the 6-party forum, to take a rightfully tough stance toward North Korea and to seriously consider proactively joining the consultation with Korea and/or the US.

On the other hand, Korea should be ambidextrous in dealing with North Korea. In other words, Korea's approach toward North Korea should not only be prompt to take a tough path, but at the same time should also be resilient enough to change from punishment to accommodation when North Korea shows genuine progress in dismantiling and/or freezing nuclear activities. From this perspective, Korea should be ready to loosen its punitive measures toward Korea, including reopening the Kaesong Industrial Complex and resuming its humanitarian assistance and economic aid to North Korea on the condition that the latter relents its provocative stance.

When it comes to the question of who will lead inter-Korea matters in the first place, the answer should be Korea, and this hard reality should guide Korean policy toward North Korea. Efforts to mitigate military tension and conciliatory measures to induce North Korea to come to the dialogue table should all be led by Korea rather than any other nations. Although Korea should have close consultation with the other 4 participants in the 6-party talk, particularly the US and China, to obtain a substantive outcome, no nation other than Korea itself is ultimately responsible for any outcomes of the inter-Korean interaction and the 6-party talk. Korea's North Korean policy should be tuned to this sobering fact.

As a multilateral forum on the North Korean nuclear issue, the now virtually defunct 6-party talk should be revived as a more effective consultation mechanism to produce visible outcomes. For that purpose, the 6-party forum should be managed in a more flexible way. For example, the 6-party talk should embrace other smaller forms of dialogue within the larger framework, such as a 3-nation talk with the participation of Korea, the US, and China. China may be reluctant to join other types of forums where North Korea is absent, but Korea should be able to persuade China to show more flexibility in order to change North Korean behavior and to make the multilateral dialogue more outcome-based.

Finally, for the purpose of inter-Korean reunification, Korea also has to work out substantive plans leading to peaceful reunification. As a first step in this venture, the 9.19 Beijing Agreement of 2005 could be resuscitated as a starting point for another round of 6-party talks to be held in the future. The agreement at the time of the deal included maximum consensus among the 6-party nations for building a peace regime.[9] In line with this, Korea should be prepared to propose its own blueprints for simultaneously pursuing North Korea denuclearization and inter-Korean reunification. Detailed and realistic preparation on the Korean side might help in creating smooth relations when an anticipated or unanticipated window of opportunity opens in the future.

8.3.5 Investing More in Public and Middle Power Diplomacy

Along with other efforts, Korea needs to pay more attention to and invest more in public diplomacy and middle power diplomacy to gain more favorable global public opinion for the Korean position regarding its foreign policy. This kind of

---

[9]As a matter of fact, during the process leading to the final 9.19 agreement in Beijing in 2005, North Korea committed itself to the verifiable denunciation of its nuclear project, and the US confirmed it has no intention of attacking North Korea. In addition, concerned parties (meaning the US and North Korea) agreed to begin discussing a process for a permanent peace regime on the Korean Peninsula within the framework of the 6-party talk. In other words, the agreement was both a plan for North Korean denuclearization and a blueprint for establishing a peace regime and paving the way for eventual Korean reunification. The agreement, however, went nowhere because above all else North Korea did not hesitate to revoke what it had committed, always claiming continued US hostile policy toward North Korea.

diplomatic effort is in urgent need given the huge public diplomacy investment by rival nations, as exemplified by Japan's public diplomacy drive to earn the hearts and minds of think tank experts and politicians in the US before Prime Minister Abe's visit to Washington in May 2015.

Specifically, Korea should invest more in public diplomacy, including ODA, for developing countries where Korean knowhow on economic development and democratization meets their needs much better than any other models of the Western experience or Japanese development do (Lee 2013: 360–361). For example, Korea should more actively promote and export the Korean experience of the New Village Movement to developing nations where farming regions are still in extreme poverty and isolated from the benefits of urban infrastructure. At the same time, Korea could also invest more in education on elections and voting in newly emerging democracies by sending administration officials and experts.

With respect to middle power diplomacy, Korea should become more deeply involved with developing nations by teaching them the skills and technologies which Korea is well-positioned to provide given the underdeveloped state of their economies and social systems. At the same time, by actively participating as a messenger in such regional forums as ASEAN+3 and EAS, Korea can deliver information regarding their needs and concerns to the other advanced powers such as the US, China, and western democracies with which Korea has multiple dialogue channels.

Furthermore, Korea needs to establish on its own a multilateral consultation mechanism between itself and developing nations to become a good listener to their concerns and to get them out of extreme poverty. The actual form can be either a multilateral organization with a large number of members or a smaller dialogue forum with several nations as members. As a leading nation that can teach past development lessons to underdeveloped countries, Korea can also utilize this type of communication mechanism to listen to their concerns and wishes, and provide realistic solutions based on its own experience through a mechanism of its own making.

8.4   Conclusion

As Korea has to face tough foreign policy challenges at the dawn of the 21st century, this article intended to identify the challenges to be seriously addressed by the Korean government, and to provide adequate recommendations for strategic responses in the future. In turn, these challenges and responses should be reviewed in the newly created conditions under which 21st century Korean diplomacy operates: the domestic political change since democratization in 1987 and the intensifying US-China rivalry in Northeast Asia.

Since the 1987 democratization, the Korean government has necessarily taken domestic repercussions into consideration when designing and implementing for-eign policy alternatives. Democratization released dormant voices into the public decision-making process, and the foreign policy area cannot be the exception. Furthermore, the information revolution made domestic elements all the more important in the foreign policy-making process, since the government can no longer monopolize information. As a result, effective foreign policy should heed domestic feedback.

Outwardly, Northeast Asian international relations have become the arena of a US-China tug-of-war since the US declared its Asian "pivoting" stance. Always sensitive to the activation of Korea-US-Japanese trilateral collaboration, China still sees North Korea as a strategic asset rather than a strategic burden. The US supports Japan's emboldened security role, anticipating that it can relieve its defense burden and work as an advance guard post watching out for Chinese expansionism and North Korean provocation. In this tough situation, Korea should avoid both leaning too much toward China and being dragged with the US and Japan into confrontation against China.

North Korean nuclear ambition should be addressed within the 6-party talk framework, but the long defunct forum needs to be more flexibly managed. Korea could be in a position to create a side forum within the 6-party talk framework, such as a consultation conference among Korea, the US, and China. From a longer-term perspective, Korea should be on alert to prevent the two giants from getting entangled in unnecessary animosity. On the other hand, to break out of the deadlock on the North Korean nuclear issue, Korea should be prepared to take initiative among the countries concerned. In addition, Korea has to prepare its own inter-Korean reunification plan to be discussed in the 6-party forum sometime in the future.

Finally, to create a friendlier milieu for Korean diplomacy, Korea should be more concerned with public and middle power diplomacy. As a nation having achieved both economic development and democratization, Korea is entitled to play a messenger role between developing and developed nations. The experience accumulated through rapid economic development and uninterrupted democratization will help Korean endeavor to implement this.

References

Chun J (ed) (2015) East Asia and the Korea Peninsula in the US-China competition. Neulbom Plus, Seoul (in Korean)

Chun J, Choo J (2013) Changes in the US-China relationship and the future of Korean foreign policy. In: Ha Y (ed) Toward 2020: ten agenda for South Korea's foreign policy. East Asia Institute, Seoul, pp 61–114 (in Korean)

Clinton H (2010) Remarks on regional architecture in Asia: principles and priorities. Honolulu, Hawaii. http://m.state.gov/md135090.htm

Clinton H (2011) America's pacific century. Honolulu, Hawaii. http://www.state.gov/secretary/20092013clinton/rm/2011/11/176999.htm

Cooper AF (1997) Niche diplomacy: middle powers after the cold war. Macmillan Press, New York

Cull N (2008) Public diplomacy: taxonomies and histories. Ann Am Acad Polit Soc Sci 616(1): 31–54

Ha Y (ed) (2013) Toward 2020: ten agenda for South Korea's foreign policy. East Asia Institute, Seoul (in Korean)

Hamm TY, Namgung G (ed) (2010) Korean foreign policy: history and agenda. Sahoepyoungron, Seoul (in Korean)

Jaung H (2008) Party politics and foreign policy making in Korea. Korean Polit Sci Rev 42(3):267–285 (in Korean)

JoongAng Daily (2015) Park appeals to Beijing on South China Sea. http://koreajoongangdaily. joins.com/news/article/Article.aspx?aid=3011908

Kim CW (2009) Middle power as unit of analysis of international relations: its conceptualizations and implications. Korean J Int Relat 49(1):7–36 (in Korean)

Korea Herald (2015) U.S. urges Korea to speak out on China Sea dispute. http://www.koreaherald. com/view.php?ud=20150604001186

Lee C (1993) The decision-making structure and players of the Korean foreign policy-making. In: Lee B, Kim EG (eds) Korean foreign policy. Bummunsa, Seoul, pp 147–182 (in Korean)

Lee H (2003) Two level games under power asymmetry: agricultural negotiations between Korea, the US and EC. Korea Int Polit 19(3):173–193 (in Korean)

Lee S (2012) South Korea as new middle power seeking complex diplomacy. EAI East Asia Security Initiative Working Paper 25

Lee S (2013) Changes in development assistance order of the 21st century and Korea. In: Ha Y (ed) Toward 2020: ten agenda for South Korea's foreign policy. East Asia Institute, Seoul, pp 329–368 (in Korean)

Lee B, Kim EG (eds) (1993) Korean foreign policy. Bummunsa, Seoul (in Korean)

Melissen J, Sohn Y (2015) Leveraging middle power public diplomacy in East Asian International relations. EAI Issue Briefing

Ministry of Foreign Affairs and Trade (2009) Six decades of Korean foreign policy: 1948–2008. Ministry of Foreign Affairs and Trade, Seoul (in Korean)

Namgung Y (2004) A critical approach to Kim Dae Jung administration's North Korea policy. Youngnam J Int Relat 7(2):26–44 (in Korean)

Nye JS Jr (2004) Soft power: the means to success in world politics. Public Affairs, New York

Obama B (2009) Remarks by President Obama at Suntory Hall. Office of the Press Secretary. https:// obamawhitehouse.archives.gov/the-press-office/remarks-president-barack-obama-suntory-hall

Yu H. (2002) Domestic politics of Korea-Chile free trade agreement negotiation: interest groups and domestic institutions in domestic negotiations. Korean Polit Sci Rev 36(3):175–197 (in Korean)

Chapter 9
Conclusion

Jongwon Choi, Huck-ju Kwon and Min Gyo Koo

9.1 Korea as a Model of Growth: Old and New

The Korean development experience is a good learning example of economic and social development for many developing countries. This involves the successful mobilization of private capacities guided by government planning and discipline, and there is no doubt that the government-led development strategy has achieved quite a lot toward eradicating poverty and sharing prosperity. Per capita income has increased from an extremely low level to a high of more than USD 25,000 in the past seven decades. As Koo notes in this volume, Korea joined the "one-trillion-dollar trading club" at the end of 2011 and became the ninth largest trading country in the world. More intriguingly, from 1945 to the late 1990s, Korea received USD 12 billion in foreign assistance and effectively used it as a catalyst for economic and social development. On January 1, 2010, it became the first ever aid-recipient-turned-member country of the Development Assistance Committee (DAC) under the umbrella of the Organization for Economic Cooperation and Development (OECD).

During the initial period of economic and social upswing, the main concerns for Korea were internally economic growth and externally security threats from North Korea. It was a significant imperative to maintain a security alliance with the US to defend against the communist threat, while competing with rival countries in the same export markets, and dealing with interventionist international organizations

J. Choi (✉) · H. Kwon · M.G. Koo
Graduate School of Public Administration, Seoul National University, Seoul, South Korea
e-mail: jwchoi@snu.ac.kr

H. Kwon
e-mail: hkwon4@snu.ac.kr

M.G. Koo
e-mail: mgkoo@snu.ac.kr

© Springer International Publishing AG 2017
J. Choi et al. (eds.), *The Korean Government and Public Policies in a Development Nexus*, The Political Economy of the Asia Pacific,
DOI 10.1007/978-3-319-52473-3_9

such as the United Nations, the World Bank, the IMF, and the ILO. Nevertheless the goal of public policy was clear: ending poverty and creating an affluent society for future generations. With this in mind, the Korean public tolerated such an authoritarian approach to economic and social development and any attempts to challenge the authority of the government were effectively suppressed.

The downsides of the Korean developmental state should not, however, obscure its achievements and continuing strengths. As noted by Choi and Choi in Chap. 2, Korea is one of the rare late industrialization countries that eventually combined rapid economic growth with a thriving democracy and social cohesion. Its industrial competitiveness is still strong and its democracy is solid, as evidenced by the peaceful transfer of power over the past three decades. For the first time in its long history, Korea's social livelihood and economic capacity is widely recognized and admired, which has resulted in high diplomatic and political visibility in the international arena.

9.2 From a Middle Income Country to a Mature Post-industrial Society

From a comparative development perspective, Korea has successfully overcome both domestic and international challenges arising after initial economic success, and avoided falling into the middle-income trap. In Chap. 5 Lee, Im, and Han explain that the national innovation system help the Korean economy upgrade its core industry with a rapid technological change. Korea became one of the leading economy in the information technology and related products in the 2000s. With industrial products based on high technology Korean government actively promoted the free trade agreements with her international trading partners. Koo characterizes Korean government's trade policy with the notion of developmental liberalism in Chap. 7.

The book has looked into political and social dimension to understand Korea's progress from the middle income country. In terms of politics, democracy was consolidated with regular and peaceful turn-overs of governments based on fair elections. Kwon points out in Chap. 3 the institutional reforms of banking transaction and property registration provided institutional infrastructure for political and economic transparency and accountability. As we have witnessed in political turmoil in many developing countries, political conflicts and civil unrests could wipe out years of economic progress in a short span of time. Political stability provided a necessary condition for Korea's progress.

It was also made clear that maintaining social cohesion was key for Korea to advance through the middle income threshold. The developmental welfare state was extended and strengthened in order to provide social protection to those falling behind in the period of economic adjustment. Kwon shows in Chap. 6 that the fragmented and selective developmental welfare state was reformed to be more inclusive. Flourishing civil society organizations channeled through different voices of society to influence public policies, according to Lee and Sung in Chap. 4.

Although it added further difficulties for the government, it helps Korean society to maintain social cohesion.

However, Korea's story also reveals that success may eventually beget failure, as repeating past actions is almost certain to lead to failure in a world of dynamic economic and political change. As noted in the article "What Do You Do When You Reach the Top?" that appeared in *The Economist* on November 12, 2011: "To outsiders, South Korea's heroic economic ascent is a template for success. But now it has almost caught up with the developed world, it must change its approach." In fact, the Korean government has attempted for the last twenty years to conceive of a new approach for future progress toward a mature post-industrial society and leader of the global community; the authors of this book have sought to assess whether and to what extent these efforts have materialized.

With the advent of democracy in the late 1980s and in the aftermath of the financial crisis in the late 1990s, the political, social and economic conditions that had underpinned Korea's traditional government-led paradigm came under great pressure. Korea now faces the triangular challenge of better economic performance, greater social cohesion, and more political accountability. While the Korean model of government-led economic development remains an example for developing countries, Korea itself now needs something new to sustain its prosperity. In Chap. 3, Kwon examines how and to what extent past governments attempted to overcome the legacies of the developmental state model in an era of democratization, as well as where they have thus far failed. He concludes that the Korean governments for the past thirty years failed to conceive a new governance idea for the future.

Reforming the big business conglomerates, the *chaebol*, can no longer be postponed or delayed as the economic and social costs have begun to exceed the benefits. Economic polarization is undermining the social fabric of Korean society. In the past, Korea fared well in combining growth with equity, but the income distribution is changing fast in favor of the richest, particularly the *chaebol*. The government has repeatedly used social policies to insulate the less-privileged from the fluctuating effects of capitalism, mainly by securing decent jobs at home and by keeping opportunities open. However, social policies often worsen the existing problems while also becoming somehow lost between conflicting goals and values. The government 'economic democratization' initiative has made absolutely no progress, and bureaucrats and politicians pass the political buck more than ever before.

The post-industrialization story of Korean transition illustrates an important point: democracy is no longer an exogenous variable in the Korean development model. Korea's maturing democracy is demanding greater accountability and transparency in the policymaking process, while requiring the government to better support entrepreneurship and innovation. Lee and Sung note in Chap. 4 that civil society organizations play a constructive role in democracy, but they also acutely point out that civil society organizations are heavily dependent on government funding. Despite the vocal presence of civil society organizations in democratic politics, a new relationship between the state and society has not been fully shaped.

9.3   Two Steps Back for One Step Forward

Building on main findings and arguments of the chapters in Part II on areas of public policy, this section critically evaluates Korea's economic and social transitions and policy adaptations in key areas: innovation policy, social policy, trade policy and foreign policy.

First of all, Korea has done well in playing catch-up. To keep growing, however, it needs a new strategy beyond simply benchmarking and emulating the world front-runners. As Lee, Im, and Han point out in Chap. 5, Korea can put itself in a better position by improving on the successes of others. But in order to sustain overall economic performance, a focus on innovation is crucial. The *chaebol* system is a double-edged sword in this regard and the Korean economy depends on it to an unhealthy degree. The 'too-big-to-fail' mentality prevents many companies from innovating in terms of business practices, and there are signs that many are actually stifling innovation and entrepreneurship by soaking up capital and talent that could have been better used by small- and medium-sized firms. When the government favors big companies, smaller ones suffer; but coddling small firms will do no good, either. As The Economist (2011) notes, except in some internet businesses and computer gaming, Korea has few start-ups and cutting-edge technology firms.

Second, Korea's developmental welfare state has become more inclusive over the years. It played an important role in steering away from the East Asian economic crisis in 1997/1998 and provided important social protection for those falling behind during the crisis. However, Kwon argues in Chap. 6 that it falls short of effectively addressing new social risks. Korea is aging more rapidly than any other industrialized country. Elderly poverty is a serious social issue that plagues Korea with higher percentages in populations over 65. Equitable income distribution previously provided a sense of social solidarity that society as a whole was benefiting from the breakneck speed of playing catch-up, but discontent with inequality is rising. As such, there is a growing demand for a universal welfare state. However, populist competition in the shadow of elections has misled many Koreans into believing that more generous welfare spending can be achieved without increasing taxes. In reality, however, a widening fiscal deficit and sluggish growth has stalled even timid welfare plans. Kwon maintains that in order to make a successful transition from a developmental welfare state to a universal welfare state, Korea should make social spending compatible with economic development, while deepening and widening the understanding of universal welfare as a basic human right.

Third, Koo begins Chap. 7 with an observation that Korea's trade policy has responded to internal challenges and external crises by repositioning, adapting, and restructuring its policy ideas and institutions. Even with greater trade liberalization, the Korean government has opted to maintain the legacies of the developmental state, with the government still playing an important role in planning, implementing, and sustaining trade reforms. Equally important, however, is the growing need for transparency in and accountability for trade liberalization, which has set the new political dynamics of policymaking and policy implementation. According to Koo, the rise and fall of the Office of the Minister for Trade (1998–2013) shows that the governance of trade policymaking and negotiations is in flux, if not in complete disarray. Korea's trade policy now faces a new dilemma between democracy and trade openness. This chapter observes that a growing proportion of the Korean public wants their government to negotiate trade treaties in a more effective and democratic manner.

Finally, Sohn evaluates Korea's foreign policy in Chap. 8. Korea remains committed to its traditional security alliance with the United States, but the most prominent feature of its foreign policy transformation is embracing China as a strategic partner. Such a policy shift is particularly intriguing because Korea has been one of the principal beneficiaries of the so-called hub-and-spoke system backed by American hegemony. The growing importance of China is twofold: economic and strategic. Economically, China has become Korea's largest trading partner, accounting for more than 25% of total trade. Many agree that Korea was able to recover from the 2008 global economic slump faster than Western countries, mainly because the Chinese market shielded the Korean market from adverse impacts. Strategically, China is becoming ever more important to Korea in order to peacefully resolve the North Korean nuclear situation and to unify the divided nation. More often than not, however, Korea's new China policy orientation is lost somewhere between bandwagoning, balancing, and hedging. The Korean hope for a tougher Chinese approach to North Korea has so far been met with disappointment, while Korea's own policy towards North Korea continues to swing back and forth between hard-lines and soft-lines. As this chapter notes, the future of Korea's foreign policy lies in 'multi-layered diplomacy,' both foreign and domestic.

9.4 What Lies Ahead

The ongoing adjustment and adaptation of South Korea's public policy defies any clear demarcation between government-led developmentalism and market-driven liberalism. But the question is not whether the government continues to lead economic development, but how it can help sustain growth and open up new possibilities for welfare, innovation, trade, and unification.

Korean democracy is praised, but not envied by its developing followers. Economic development and democracy are not mutually exclusive. Democracy may have a negative impact on economic and social transitions in the short-run, possibly due to the exacerbation of distributional conflicts. However, as the Korean case shows, democracy is likely to induce better economic performance, greater social cohesion, and more political accountability in the long-run.

Korean democracy has advanced over the past three decades and now stands on a solid foundation. But it has yet to complete the tripod of democracy: political freedom, economic prosperity, and social justice. There are several prerequisites concerning government policies that must be met. Meeting these goals will be a daunting task as the 2016 political scandal caused by the President herself and her close confidante has severely damaged the credibility of the Korean government.

First, sheltering and protecting domestic firms, both small and large, will only make them less efficient and damage competitiveness. Many in Korea still focus on the question of prioritizing growth or distribution. This is indeed a chicken-or-egg causality dilemma, but the bottom line is that without creating wealth through industrial competitiveness, no one can afford to share anything.

Second, the potential of the welfare state to create human capital and competitiveness should be further exploited in the context of post-industrial society (The Economist 2016a). The Korean government also needs to see the potential of social service facilities for economic development and social cohesion. These include public childcare, elderly care services and adult education and training institutions. At the same time, it is necessary to avoid making populist social promises to earn political support.

Third, the *chaebol* system is at the core of economic and social inequality. The 'economic democratization' election campaign slogan should go beyond political rhetoric, but the government is not in a position to make any real changes. A bottom-up approach is therefore necessary to restore a healthy check-and-balance mechanism. Fourth, administrative reform under the auspices of the 'new public management' paradigm should be critically reassessed. As the authors in the preceding chapters have emphasized, there have been serious mismatches between goals and practices. Despite a series of reform efforts, successive governments have failed to depart from old governance practices. An outdated, paternalistic paradigm is no longer compatible with a maturing democracy.

Finally, although the incumbent President maintains that "unification is a bonanza," the government as a whole seems under-prepared for the sudden collapse of North Korea, both financially and diplomatically. A new development paradigm should endogenize the unification factor, as an increasingly unstable North Korea could cause tremendous problems for South Korea. The costs of reunion would be staggering: by conservative estimates about $1 trillion, or three-quarters of Korea's annual GDP. The vast expense of German unification would pale in comparison (The Economist 2011, 2016b). Aside from fiscal and social preparations, Korea's unification diplomacy should be better organized. To create a friendlier milieu for unification diplomacy, Korea should be more concerned with public and middle power diplomacy.

In this book, we have examined the pathways Korea has taken in overcoming the middle-income threshold, and discussed policy efforts to enter a new development period on the way to becoming a mature post-industrial society. Although there were difficult moments along the way, it is fair to say that Korea has managed well. This is at least partly because Korea has flown as part of the flying geese, following the leading nations. However, as the county makes its way to the front, it will be necessary to play a larger role in determining future directions. This book finds that Korea has been struggling to carry out the task, but we are nevertheless optimistic about the future of the country.

References

The Economist (2011) South Korea's economy: what do you do when you reach the top? http://www.economist.com/node/21538104

The Economist (2016a) Social welfare in South Korea: doubt of the benefit. http://www.economist.com/news/asia/21695926-local-experiment-expand-handouts-ruffles-central-government-doubt-benefit?zid=306&ah=1b164dbd43b0cb27ba0d4c3b12a5e227

The Economist (2016b) Korea opportunities: what North and South Korea would gain if they were reunified. http://www.economist.com/blogs/graphicdetail/2016/05/korea-opportunities

Erratum to: The Korean Government and Public Policies in a Development Nexus

Jongwon Choi, Huck-ju Kwon and Min Gyo Koo (Eds.)

Erratum to:
J. Choi et al. (eds.), *The Korean Government and Public Policies in a Development Nexus*, **The Political Economy of the Asia Pacific, DOI 10.1007/978-3-319-52473-3**

The original version of the book was inadvertently published without the volume number in the cover and title page. The erratum book has been updated with the change.

The updated original online version for this book can be found at http://dx.doi.org/10.1007/978-3-319-52473-3

© Springer International Publishing AG 2017
J. Choi et al. (eds.), *The Korean Government and Public Policies in a Development Nexus*, The Political Economy of the Asia Pacific,
DOI 10.1007/978-3-319-52473-3_10

The manufacturer's authorised representative in the EU is Springer
Nature Customer Service Centre GmbH, Europaplatz 3, 69115 Heidelberg,
Germany. If you have any concerns regarding our products, please
contact ProductSafety@springernature.com

Printed and bound by CPI Group (UK) Ltd, Croydon, CR0 4YY
30/04/2026
02100216-0004